One day Jesus left the crowds to pray alone.
Only his disciples were with him, and he asked them,
'Who do people say I am?'

(Luke 9.18 NLT)

Contents

List of contributors

Julian Baggini

Philosopher, journalist and co-founder of *The Philosophers'
Magazine*. Author of *The Godless Gospel: Was Jesus a great
moral teacher?* (Granta 2020), *How the World Thinks: A global
history of philosophy* (Granta 2019) and *A Short History of Truth:
Consolations for a post-truth world* (Quercus 2017).

Terry Eagleton

Distinguished Professor of English Literature, Lancaster University. Author of *Radical Sacrifice* (Yale 2018), *Reason, Faith
and Revolution* (Yale 2009), and *The Meaning of Life: A very
short introduction* (OUP 2007).

Robin Gill

Emeritus Professor of Applied Theology, University of Kent, and
editor of the journal *Theology*. Author of *Christian Ethics: The
Basics* (Routledge 2020), *Society Shaped by Theology* (Routledge
2013) and *Moral Passion and Christian Ethics* (CUP 2017), and editor of *The Cambridge Companion to Christian Ethics* (CUP 2011).

Amy-Jill Levine

University Professor of New Testament and Jewish Studies and
Mary Jane Werthan Professor of Jewish Studies, Vanderbilt
Divinity School and Department of Jewish Studies. Co-author
of *The Gospel of Luke* (CUP 2018), co-editor of *The Jewish
Annotated New Testament* (OUP 2017), author of *Short Sto-
ries by Jesus: The Enigmatic Parables of a Controversial Rabbi*

(HarperOne 2014) and *The Misunderstood Jew: The Church and the Scandal of the Jewish Jesus* (HarperOne 2006).

Tarif Khalidi

Professor of Islamic and Arabic Studies, American University of Beirut; formerly Professor of Arabic and a fellow of King's College, Cambridge. Translator of *The Qur'an* (Penguin Classics 2013), and author of *Images of Muhammad* (Doubleday 2009) and *The Muslim Jesus* (Harvard 2003).

Nick Spencer

Senior Fellow, Theos. Author of *The Evolution of the West* (SPCK 2016), *Atheists: The origins of the species* (Bloomsbury 2014) and *Darwin and God* (SPCK 2009).

Joan E. Taylor

Professor of Christian Origins and Second Temple Judaism, King's College London. Author of *What Did Jesus Look Like?* (Bloomsbury 2018) and editor of *Jesus and Brian: Exploring the historical Jesus and his times via Monty Python's 'Life of Brian'* (Bloomsbury 2015).

Rowan Williams

Master of Magdalene College, Cambridge and 104th Archbishop of Canterbury (2002–12). Author of *Christ the Heart of Creation* (Bloomsbury 2018), *God with Us: The meaning of the cross and resurrection – then and now* (SPCK 2017) and *Meeting God in Mark* (SPCK 2014).

A. N. Wilson

Novelist, journalist and broadcaster. Author of *The Mystery of Charles Dickens* (Atlantic 2020), *Charles Darwin: Victorian Mythmaker* (John Murray 2017) and *The Book of the People: How to Read the Bible* (Atlantic 2015).

Introduction

TOM HOLLAND

His coming was foretold by prophecy and his birth heralded by miracles. Only narrowly did he escape a massacre of the innocents. Laying claim to the great mission of his life, he received the blessing of his divine father. Gathering followers drawn from obscurity about him, he scorned the pretensions of monarchs. He condemned those who had offended against his father to a place of wailing and gnashing of teeth; he preached to a war-ravaged world a message of brotherhood and peace. Many rejected him, but many accepted him as their Lord. In the end, not even death could hold him in its chains. Cheating the tomb, he rose and ascended into heaven. There, seated at the right hand of his father, he reigned in divine majesty. Meanwhile, on earth, his disciples did not forget their risen Saviour. Across the known world, the memory of him was cherished in people's hearts. This, so it was proclaimed in Galatia and in Thessalonia, in Corinth and in Rome, was *euangelion*: 'good news'.

At once a man and a god, mortal and immortal, Augustus Caesar stood at the centre of the fastest growing cult the world had ever seen. The very name awarded him by his countrymen proclaimed his ambivalent status as a human being who had simultaneously partaken of the divine. '*Augustus* is what our fathers call anything holy. *Augustus* is what we call a temple that has been properly consecrated by the hand of the priests.'[1] To worship him as a god was to consecrate one of the great convulsions in world history. His rise to power amid the implosion of Rome's traditional republican form of government was an authentically transformational moment. Ronald Syme, in his classic account of the process, went so far as to describe it as the 'Roman revolution'. Over the course of many decades, a people who had always defined themselves by their contempt for kings were brought to submit to the rule of a general, an *imperator*, who had been victorious in almost everything he did. Augustus, as an *imperator*, an 'emperor', wielded power that was indeed of a revolutionary order. The dominion he governed was vast beyond the dreams of a Pharaoh, and the armed forces he had at his command were on a scale fit to have put Alexander's in the shade. Never before in history had any man enjoyed such fame across such an immense expanse of the world. Within Augustus' own lifetime, no living Roman had ever appeared on a coin minted in Rome; yet by the time of his death, the face of Caesar had become familiar in even the remotest corners of the Empire, wherever money might be handled, and taxes demanded. 'Whose likeness and inscription is this?' Itinerant street preachers in Galilee might ask the question and know the answer.

Yet Augustus, for all the novelty of the order that he founded, did not care to cast himself as a revolutionary. *Novae res* – "new things" – were regarded by most Romans with deep suspicion. Augustus himself, who in almost everything save the scale of his ambition was deeply conservative, had far too much respect for tradition to proclaim a year zero. In the wake of the civil wars that had brought him to power, during the session of the Senate that saw the decree passed which defined him as *'Augustus'*, there were some senators who had pushed for him to be given an alternative name: Romulus. The allusion was to Rome's founder, the man after whom the city was named. There was to be no second founding, however. Augustus had no wish to recalibrate the Romans' understanding of time, which numbered years *ab urbe condita*: 'from the founding of the city'. There could be only the one Romulus, only the one starting point for the city. The revolution over which Augustus presided was – if a revolution at all – like the turning of a wheel.

The centuries passed. The world did not stay still. Rome's rule over the western half of her empire melted away. Rome itself was sacked. Barbarians planted their kingdoms in what had once been imperial provinces. In one of these, a realm named Northumbria, in a library close to the crumbling fortifications that once, centuries previously, had constituted the frontier of Roman Britain, a scholar by the name of Bede set himself to fashioning a new understanding of time. Rome's fall had not prevented chroniclers from continuing to use the formula *ab urbe condita*, and Bede, steeped in the learning of his predecessors as he was, employed it readily. Yet it left him dissatisfied. Seven centuries on from the lifetime of Augustus, he could see – infinitely more clearly than the emperor himself had done – that the fulcrum of time was indeed to be identified with a point in his reign. Drawing on calendrical tables compiled some two centuries earlier by a scholar from the Black Sea, Bede began to measure years from this same point: *anno Domini*, in the year of the Lord.

The *Dominus*, however, was not Augustus. By Bede's lifetime, the memory of the emperor had become a hazy one, blotted out by the blaze of a very different man. This Lord had not ruled an empire, nor commanded armies, nor had his face minted on coins. Instead, he had been born in the utmost obscurity, lived a life tramping roads and fields, and died a squalid death, nailed to a cross, a convicted criminal. Yet his death had not at all been what it might have seemed. So, at any rate, in Northumbria, it had come to be believed. There, when a poet saw a cross in his dreams, he could know that it was no '*fracodes gealga*' – no 'felon's gallows'. The implement of torture that to the Romans had symbolized the power of the conqueror over the conquered, of the strong over the weak, of the master over the slave, had been transformed, in the imaginings of the Northumbrians, into the very opposite. The paradox of Augustus Caesar, the warlord who had become a god, could not compare with the paradox of Jesus Christ, whose birth in the reign of Augustus as a subject of the Roman state had marked – so Bede believed – the moment on which all of history turned, and who, by his agonizing death, had served to redeem mankind. The cross, that terrible gallows, had become a tree of glory.

> At the fair sight, I saw that lively beacon
> Changing its clothes and hues; sometimes it was
> Bedewed with blood and drenched with flowing gore,
> At other times it was bedecked with treasure.[2]

No wonder, then, that the figure of Jesus should have haunted Northumbrian dreams.

Today, a millennium and more since the time of Bede and the author of 'The Dream of the Rood', he lives in the dreams of more people than ever before. Across the planet, over two billion believe that Jesus was indeed the Son of God, Light of Light, very God of very God. The impact he has had on history, however, is not to be measured solely by such a statistic. It is to be found as well, for instance, in the very understanding of "revolution" that suffuses this book. When Ronald Syme, back in the 1930s, wrote his great study of Augustus, he knew perfectly well that the word possessed rich shades of signification that would have been incomprehensible to the Romans. 'The subject of this book', he wrote on 1 June 1939, 'is the transformation of state and society at Rome between 60 BC and AD 14'.[3] At such a moment of history, Syme had no need to be reminded that there existed regimes in the world that upheld a very different understanding of what "revolution" might mean. Just over two decades previously, the tsar of all the Russians, a man whose title derived by virtue of a lengthy and much punctuated line of descent from Augustus, had been shot by revolutionaries committed to the conviction that the last were to be first, and the first last. The ambition of the Bolsheviks to build heaven on earth, despite the stern insistence of their ideologues that 'in practice, no less than in theory, communism is incompatible with religious faith',[4] was nothing if not itself an expression of religious faith. That the rich stood condemned to woe; that the poor and the hungry were to be redeemed from their miseries; that all the world was irrevocably destined to be brought to a time of judgement: all these convictions of the Bolsheviks, however disguised they might be by talk of dialectical materialism, derived ultimately from the teachings of Jesus. If, as Marx and Lenin had insisted, communism offered humanity a liberation from Christianity, then it was one that seemed eerily like a recalibration of it.

Yet if there were revolutionaries whose attitudes to Christ were profoundly oedipal, then so also were there others whose repudiation of his teachings was absolute. *The Roman Revolution* – published a week after the outbreak of the Second World War – had been profoundly influenced in its attitude to Augustus by the uses to which the figure of the emperor had been put by the two fascist regimes of Italy and Germany. Mussolini, the *Duce* who cast himself as a new Caesar, had made predictable play with the second millenary of Augustus' birth in 1938, but so too, perhaps more surprisingly, had Hitler. The Führer, who evinced little but contempt for the fascination felt by many of his lieutenants for the ancient Germans, identified instead with the potency and the glamour of the superpower that had sought in vain to conquer the German tribes: the Roman Empire. In particular, he identified with Augustus.

He visited the exhibition staged by Mussolini to celebrate the 2000th birthday of Rome's first emperor twice, and had his propagandists assiduously promote comparisons between the two of them. Roman history, so he had opined in *Mein Kampf,* was the best teacher that an aspirant world conqueror could possibly hope to have. The lessons that it taught were valuable precisely because they served to counteract what Hitler, by the time that war broke out, had come to see as the heaviest blow ever struck against humanity. Rotten through with Jewish resentment of the strong and the beautiful, Christ's teachings had affected the German people like syphilis, leaving them sick with compassion for the weak, the sick, the imbecilic. The Führer, Goebbels noted in his diary in 1941, regarded the legacy of Jesus not just with suspicion, but also with hatred: it had served to cripple all that was noblest in humanity. The freedom and the happiness that once, back in the palmy days of the Greeks and the Romans, had been the prerogatives of the healthy and the strong, to the benefit of both peoples, had been blotted out. 'What a difference between the benevolent, smiling Zeus and the pain-wracked, crucified Christ.'[5]

The Third Reich was Europe's first erstwhile Christian state since the Viking period to reject not just confessional Christianity, but the very fundamentals of Christian teaching: the conviction that all human beings have been created equal; the assumption that the strong and healthy have a duty of care to the weak and the sick. The unique status that the Nazis hold in our contemporary demonology, and perhaps especially the role that Hitler plays as the quintessence of evil, serve, then, as backhanded compliments to the enduring significance of Christ in a West that has come, over the past decades, increasingly to abandon confessional Christianity. Likewise, the admiration that Hitler felt for the achievements of Augustus, together with the contempt that he felt for the teachings and example of Jesus, provide a suggestive perspective on the degree to which Christianity did indeed rank as a cuckoo in the Roman nest. It is not necessary to accept Hitler's own estimation of himself as a new Augustus, nor the dark foreboding expressed by Simone Weil in 1938 that 'the analogy between the systems of Hitler and of ancient Rome is so striking that one might believe that Hitler alone, after two thousand years, has understood how to copy the Romans',[6] to recognize this. That the peoples of the Roman Empire came to worship as the Son of God not a warlord who had ruled them as emperor but a man who had suffered death at the hands of its soldiers was the marker of as profound a transformation in the understanding of power as any in human history. Christianity, of course, did not prevent emperors from continuing to claim a supernaturally sanctioned sway for themselves, nor conquerors from leading armies into war, nor the wealthy from riding past beggars without giving them a second glance, nor the educated from sitting in judgement on the wretched and the poor – but it did increasingly, over the course of the centuries, and to a degree ultimately so profound that it has come to transfigure the very essence of the Western understanding of "human nature", give reproof to their consciences. What would Jesus have done? We are all of us in the West – believers and non-believers alike – shaped by the answers that for two thousand years have been given to that question. If this does not constitute a revolution, then it is hard to know what would.

Justifiably, then, in his essay for this collection, does Nick Spencer advance a striking claim.

There can be no serious doubt that Jesus Christ is the single most important figure in at least Western, arguably world, history, his minor movement creeping through and then transforming the ancient world like some kind of metaphysical plague, which was pretty much what ancient and modern critics claim that it was.

Swelling the impact that Jesus has had on the patterns of thought of billions is the fact that, as Tarif Khalidi reminds us, the man who stands as the fountainhead of Christianity is also loved and respected by Muslims as a prophet of Islam. Clearly, the influence of a man who can feature as a manifestation of the divine in one corpus of scripture and as a prophet in another is not one that can readily be quantified. As both Julian Baggini and Rowan Williams point out, albeit from radically opposed perspectives, the name 'Jesus' can signify such a wide range of meanings to such a wide range of people – as indeed it has done for two millennia – that there is not the slightest prospect of ever purging it of ambiguity or paradox. This in itself, of course, is nothing exceptional. Augustus, another man who was hailed as a god, wore a ring with the image of a sphinx on it, and was portrayed by one of his successors as a chameleon. As Williams brilliantly points out:

> the problem is not that the history of Jesus is difficult to access, overlaid as it is by the literary and theological reception of his story; in one important sense every historical figure is a *literary* figure, encountered through the medium of how others made sense of them.

Yet this, in the case of Jesus, is merely to shift the terms of the debate: for to talk of the Jesus of literature is above all to talk of the Jesus of the four canonical gospels. Whether drawn from life or a complete work of fiction, the portrait of Christ they collectively provide constitutes what must surely rank as the most influential literary achievement in history. Written in often inelegant Greek though they may be, they furnish a portrait of someone whom generations of people, many of them living in lands undreamed of by the evangelists themselves, have for two thousand years accepted as someone at once mortal and divine, man and true God, a Jew who trod the dusty roads of Galilee and the One Creator through whom all things were made.

Such a figure could never have been convincing had he failed to convey a sense of the uncanny: of the familiar rendered mysterious. As essays by Joan Taylor, Robin Gill and Amy-Jill Levine all expertly demonstrate, the revolutionary quality of the Gospels depends in part at least on the way in which teachings that would have been perfectly familiar to Jesus' listeners alternate with commandments that must have struck them as profoundly strange, and parables dependent on subversive simile. Their potency, Levine argues, is no less today than when they were first narrated. 'Short stories that make us think, that make us question ethics and economics, need and desire, justice and vengeance, our ancestral texts and our present relations, can revolutionize the way we live'. Yet if Jesus' teachings can convincingly be portrayed as timeless, then so also is it a crucial aspect of their influence that they have been understood, over the course of the centuries and the millennia, in many and often conflicting ways. So it is that A. N. Wilson can point out in his essay that:

> No one in the pages of the Fourth Gospel, or of the Synoptics, calls for better living conditions for the Galilean villagers, better education for the Palestinian children, improvements in diet or medicinal supplies for the poorer parts of Jerusalem. . .

So it is also that Terry Eagleton can find in the life and death of Christ a model of behaviour that has provided a template for more recent radicals.

In the end, Jesus was killed because he spoke out fearlessly for love and justice in a political world, which finds such things deeply threatening. He was, in short, a martyr, one who gives up his life as a precious gift to others, like Martin Luther King or Steve Biko.

Two thousand and twenty years after the birth of Christ, we remain the children of the Christian revolution: the most disruptive, the most influential and the most enduring revolution in history. Attempts to rebrand *"anno Domini"* as the "Common Era" no more signal the exhaustion of its current than the culverting of a great river serves as a dam. The event that Bede saw as constituting the one fixed point amid the great sweep of the aeons, the only pivot, remains in this, our secular age, the enduring marker of a sense of a new beginning: the year zero of revolution.

Notes

Introduction

1 Ovid. *Fasti*: 1.609-10
2 'The Dream of the Rood', translated by Richard Hamer, in *A Choice of Anglo-Saxon Verse*, p. 165
3 Ronald Syme, *The Roman Revolution* (Oxford, 1939), p. vii
4 N. Bukharin and E. Preobrazhensky. *The ABC of Communism* (London, 2007), p. 235
5 Josef Goebbels: *The Goebbels Diaries, 1939-1941*, trans. Fred Taylor (London, 1982), p. 305
6 Simone Weil: *Selected Essays, 1934-1943*, trans. Richard Rees (Oxford, 1962), p. 96

Jesus and the mechanics
of empowerment

JOAN E. TAYLOR

In October 2011 something remarkable happened down the
street from where I work in London, in a place where I least
expected. As a teacher of Christian Origins at King's College
London, I had often asked my students to be alert to anything
in the public sphere, especially in the media, that might have
relevance for their studies, because in looking at Jesus and the
Bible as a whole there are innumerable resonances in current
culture and politics. I said this regularly to my Masters class
focusing on the Passion narratives in the Gospels, a class in
which we considered the final week of Jesus' life, including
his dramatic overturning of the money changers' tables in the
Jerusalem Temple. Jesus stated that the 'house of prayer for all
nations' had been turned into 'a cave of brigands'.[1]

Protesters occupied the area in front of St. Paul's Cathedral, calling for an end to the culture of corporate greed
and banking immorality, and Jesus' action suddenly took
on a striking contemporary relevance. As some among the
cathedral authorities fretted at the presence of protesters on
their doorstep and worried about health and safety issues,
debate ignited on which side of the stand-off Jesus would have
stood. The cathedral authorities teetered on the boundary,
being ethically on the side of the protesters in their critiques
and yet concerned about the heritage site of the building and
the orderly running of its services. Television news showed
St. Paul's dramatically closing its doors, for the first time

1

since the Second World War. That image was crushing to many Christians both inside the cathedral and worldwide, prompting serious questions to be asked. The protesters put up a banner in front of the cathedral: 'What would Jesus do?' It was photographed and printed in hundreds of newspapers and circulated via internet sites.

The ensuing debate was both illuminating and depressing. Either side, it seemed, could claim Jesus. On the one hand, it was clear that the Gospels showed that Jesus was not exactly pleased with those who heartlessly hoarded money, but on the other, it was said that Jesus' concerns were other-worldly: I heard a cleric on the radio state that his kingdom was 'not of this world' and he did not take sides, seeking only reconciliation of sinful humanity with God through his sacrificial death.

But perhaps what was remarkable was that it was considered important at all to ask the question about what Jesus would do, given that modern Britain is renowned for being a very secular (if not growingly atheistic) society, in which such religious questions were not really expected to come up. Christianity, to many people, is a bunch of myths wrapped around a core that would have you feeling bad about yourself. It is an ideological system of oppression furthering anti-scientific agendas, in cahoots with global capitalism and climate deniers, advocating discrimination against female and LGBTQ+ people.

However, the banner goes to show something. Regardless of your beliefs, and regardless of what so-called Christianity can be about now, Jesus is remembered as being in some way a figure owned by the protesters as much as by the church authorities. His message has sung out over the centuries, no matter what the packaging has been and is. There are still people out there who get it.

In my view, Jesus was quite fierce in speaking out against those in power, and very much of this world and concerned with it. He was a man of his time, using a worldview and beliefs his community held in a way that galvanized people into action. His was a message of transformation on earth. What he did and said empowered himself and others, by means of key, practical steps, so that he and his disciples could speak to the powerful. And he did take sides.

Being me

Before I go on though I would like to introduce myself briefly, since I am of the school that thinks that our interpretation of things biblical and historical is partly indebted to where we are in terms of our own worldviews. I am God-trusting, as long as 'God' is defined along the lines of *Being* and not *Old Man up in the Sky*. I map this concept on to the ultimate in other religious and philosophical systems, from Allah to Brahman to Ultimate Reality. I prefer to talk about 'trust' rather than 'faith' or 'belief', because the Greek word for both, *pistis*, indicates a fundamental trust in something real, rather than a 'belief', say, in fairies. I consider Jesus to be 'Christ', since the word 'Christ' (Messiah, literally 'anointed one') means 'King', and I see him as the king of all prophets.[2] He was a visionary empowered by God, though he lived in very different times and his belief system needs translating. I also have a sense of his continuing "livingness", experientially, and that's just a total mystery.

To call Jesus 'Saviour' is for me to say he rescues people from a life of meaninglessness. My type of 'Christianity' is therefore existentialist and humanistic. When I participate in worship that uses traditional Christian terms and rituals, I translate them, and it opens up a reality that can be profoundly moving and important. I find meaning in the symbolism of the Church's creeds and liturgies because they say something meaningful about God, humanity and community, and what the disciples of Jesus should be doing in the world. Usually, though, I prefer to sit in mindful, silent contemplation in Quaker meetings.

I think we live at a critical time when our religious systems, once integrated within different cultures, have been brought together in a global soup, and are faltering or becoming extreme and sectarian. This is not true for every part of the world, because the old systems can still have much meaning (partly dependent on the integrity of cultures or sub-cultures), but everywhere I go I meet people who say they have 'spiritual' understandings, but they do not participate institutionally, and feel annoyed with or removed from organized religion. Yet people have this sense that Jesus was important, and inspirational, and on the side of the marginalized and powerless, which is why that banner was raised in the London protests of 2011. The Church might not matter so much, to many, but Jesus still does. He can be claimed by people who want to change the world.

This understanding is founded on the teaching *of* Jesus, rather than on the teaching *about* Jesus. And I really think his was a profound message.

Being Jesus

In a nutshell, Jesus was a Jewish man who lived in Galilee, in what is now Israel, in the first century. Galilee at this time was part of the Roman Empire, ruled by a client ruler Herod Antipas. The Gospels tell us that Jesus went out to be immersed in the River Jordan by someone called John, known as 'the Baptist', who attracted huge crowds when he proclaimed an imminent transformation of the world order and called Jews to a radically ethical lifestyle, repentance and purification in preparation for the change. After John was arrested by Antipas (around 28-30 CE), Jesus spread his own message of this coming transformation, the 'Kingdom of God'. Jesus combined his teaching with astonishing healings and miraculous actions. Huge crowds gathered to hear him and be healed. He travelled around Galilee with a band of disciples, both men and women, taught them how to live according to his ideal, and sent out a group called 'the Twelve' as his representatives (apostles) to spread the message quickly and to heal in his name.

After John was executed by Antipas, Jesus set his sights on Jerusalem, with an awareness that he would be killed there. Jesus went with his disciples to the festival of Passover. As he came into Jerusalem he was greeted with great celebration. He then protested in the Temple by overturning the tables of the money changers and sellers of sacrifices, but the authorities were afraid to arrest him because of his popularity. He was betrayed by one of the Twelve, Judas Iscariot, who pointed out his secret lodgings in Gethsemane to the authorities, and who identified him there in the middle of the night by kissing him in front of the militia sent to arrest him. He was taken to the house of the High Priest, Caiaphas, in the middle of the night, where he was interrogated and beaten, passed over to the Roman governor, Pontius Pilate, who sentenced him to flogging and crucifixion, and executed by crucifixion: a Roman method of torturing someone to death by nailing them alive to hang on pieces of wood. This was done at a place, outside the city walls, called Golgotha, early on a Friday morning. He was dead not much more than 12 hours after the time of his arrest, at a time when most people were celebrating Passover and forbidden by Jewish law to bear arms.

The stories of the Gospels do not end here. On the third day after he died, resurrected Jesus was experienced by some of the disciples, and the Gospels end with an assertion of triumph: Jesus, killed by the powers of this world, was dead no longer.

You would think all this might appear in some ancient history book as a peculiar legend of a local hero. But there was something about Jesus, and the significance of his story, that has carried it through the ages.

As I try to imagine the real historical events, and the people involved in this story, I strive to understand the ancient reality, the folk beliefs, the economic situation, the ordinary life of people and how the gospel narratives came to be. I cannot explore all these things here. The main question I want to ask is how Jesus managed to do what he did. How did he change the world? What were the mechanics of empowerment he used that meant his story was not just a small footnote in the history of Rome?

Observing the empire

By "mechanics of empowerment" I mean practical actions that shift authority from currently powerful people to those who are not. One of the things I think about is Jesus as a young man, before the great story of his adult life began with John the Baptist. I think of Jesus living in the small, rural village of Nazareth, in Galilee, working as a builder or craftsman in wood or stone (*tektōn*). When I visited Nazareth a few years ago with my family, I looked out at the hills around the central valley and stream where Jesus' village was and thought how Jesus would have looked at this very shape of hills. They reminded me of my homeland, New Zealand. In some ways, growing up in Nazareth would have been like growing up in rural New Zealand, and I well remember how very far we felt from the rest of the world before the internet and jumbo jets.

Judaea, where Galilee was located, was part of a colonial enterprise: Rome was economically and militarily in charge. So what do you do, as a young man in Nazareth, if you see suffering among the people around you: people begging on the streets, hunger, widespread disease and poor health, injustices of law, huge inequalities between the estate owners and the labourers on the land, when Herod Antipas collects taxes designed not for public services but to build palaces, when the rich are totally in charge, and your religious leaders appear to accept and benefit from the situation? What do you do when around the time you were born a Roman army had come to your nearest city, Sepphoris, (when the population joined a revolt) and destroyed it, selling its inhabitants into slavery? Rebuilt and resettled during your childhood, it was now called *Autocratoris*, "City of the Autocrat", the autocrat being the Roman emperor.[3] This was just across from Nazareth, 11 km away.

The Roman emperor was not a ruler in any modern sense: his rule was not just about power, military might and economic hegemony, or a cult of personality; his rule was a religion. There were Roman imperial cult temples in Caesarea, Caesarea Philippi and Sebaste. Jews were given exemptions from direct participation in the imperial cult because of their ancestral religion, but sacrifices for the imperial family in the Jewish Temple in Jerusalem were made every day.[4] In Caesarea the focus was a massive sculpture of the goddess Roma and another of Augustus, enthroned, as Olympian Zeus. On coinage, the emperor is proclaimed "Divi f(ilius)": God's Son. When Pontius Pilate arrived as Roman prefect, he had even attempted to install shields venerated as part of the imperial cult in Jerusalem, right in the centre of the city in the royal palace where he lived. Only major protests had stalled his actions.[5]

Having a vision

So when I read the story of Jesus coming to John the Baptist and having a powerful spiritual experience, or vision, on coming up out of the water of the River Jordan, I think it needs to be understood fundamentally against the political and social backdrop of Roman rule in Judaea and the Empire as a whole. The Roman Empire was a huge trading network in which peace and prosperity were founded on a status quo of hierarchy, with top down leadership and no allowance for any criticism whatsoever: such criticism was treason (*maiestas*), and treason was a kind of sacrilege.[6] Even an eminent and elite Roman philosopher like Seneca could get offside with rulers, and be killed. What about someone from rural Galilee?

We are told in the narrative of the oldest gospel, Mark (written around 70 CE):

And it happened in those days that Jesus came from Nazareth in Galilee and was immersed in the Jordan by John, and immediately coming up from out of the water he saw the heavens splitting open and the Spirit descending like a dove into him, and a voice came from the heavens – 'You are my son, the beloved one; in you I am well pleased' (Mark 1.9-11).

You are my son – not the emperor Tiberius. *You are the beloved one.* Both terms reflect royal appointment.[7] Jesus also experiences a powerful vision – that the Spirit of God has come down from the sky like a dove, and has gone *into him.*

It is like a scene in a movie in which an ordinary guy in a small town suddenly gains a superpower. The prophet John the Baptist had predicted that someone would come after him who would be much greater than he, who would immerse people in Holy Spirit (Mark 1:8), and then bang: Jesus himself, immersed in the water, sees Holy Spirit ripping out of the great blue canopy of the sky/heaven[8] and flying like a bird down into him. The Spirit is inside him now. In hearing the voice of God identifying him, he has been commissioned to act, 'anointed' by God as his representative on earth. What is he going to do?

The Holy Spirit (a feminine term in Aramaic, Jesus' language) is the agency of God, the healing power and wisdom and foresight of God, a pure and undefiled (virginal) energy that comes into holy people and prophets.[9] In some of the early Christian tradition, Jesus is remembered as calling the Spirit his 'Mother'.[10] Prophets in ancient Israel were believed to be able to prophesy because the Spirit of God dwelt within them, and they could then do miraculous things, like healing people. Jesus would have been steeped in stories from Scripture: Elijah's raising of the widow's son, Isaiah's insistence on ethics and care for the disadvantaged, Moses' miracles and his leading of the nation of Israel out of captivity in Egypt. Prophets like Jeremiah or Amos or Nahum challenged rulers and bad ethics, and the Holy Spirit was inside them, speaking and acting through them. In the Scriptures, they were the real heroes, not kings and queens, warning Israel that good actions counted for more with God than sacrifices and rituals, prayers, conquests and worldly power.

So, in the story of Jesus' baptism by John, the mechanics of empowerment involve Jesus coming from nowhere and gaining divine power. God's voice gives Jesus a voice in a world in which only the rich and powerful had their statements heeded and recorded. In the Gospel of Mark, nothing is stated about Jesus before he came to John at the Jordan, but the implication is that prior to Jesus' baptism he does not have any Holy Spirit dwelling inside him (there is no miraculous birth story). And what Jesus experiences here is told from his point of view: 'he saw' the heavens splitting open. Unless we suppose that the whole thing is made up, the only plausible way that anyone would have known about this story is because Jesus told it to them, so we have this small window into something Jesus experienced and talked about as foundational for himself. From here on in, he was God's son, the beloved one. From the moment Jesus is immersed in the Jordan and receives the Spirit, one suspects he is not going to be a very cooperative and docile person in the Roman Empire. From a nobody from Nazareth, Jesus is about to become the biggest somebody in the world.

Having another vision

According to Mark, 'immediately the Spirit threw him into the wilderness, and he remained there for 40 days, and he was tempted by Satan'.[11] The Spirit is in charge of Jesus. It is no longer he alone, making his own decisions; this provides again a sense of empowerment, in that your behaviour is now dictated by God, not your own will. Your own will is not eradicated, however. Later on in the Gospel of Mark, there is a sense that Jesus' own will could even query the path he was on: at Gethsemane, near his disciples (before they fall asleep), he prays to his Father that the 'cup' of torture and death would pass from him, but, agonizing, he accepts in the end that it is necessary.[12] Right after his baptismal vision, though, Jesus is cast out to the wilderness by the Spirit, for his own will to be tested. Does he have the strength?

What happens next, in terms of the mechanics of empowerment, is told in a story common to the Gospels of Matthew and Luke, whereby Jesus goes to the wilderness to be 'tempted' by Satan. During the vision (or vision cluster) in the wilderness, Satan is like the spokesman for the imperial programme and worldly authority. You can use your superpower to get whatever food you want. You can rely on God/the angels to look after you. And you can get massive worldly power: 'the devil took him to a very high mountain and showed him all the kingdoms of the world and their splendour. "All this I will give to you," he said, "if you will bow down and worship me"'.[13]

By implication, Satan is in charge of the world and can give it to whomever he wants. Those who gain domination over all the kingdoms of the world have therefore been gifted these by Satan, who can pass them to his chosen ones. The world is a place in which you can have power and wealth, if you let Satan have his way. It turns out, then, that Rome must itself be in league with Satan to be the Empire it is.

This is another story that could only have been known if Jesus had told it about himself in some way. Just as he would tell parables (small allegorical stories) to teach people during his travels, he seems to have told stories about himself. He was a visionary who could have direct conversations with Satan, hearing his voice as much as he could hear the voice of God. In the end of the encounter, the temptation, Jesus defeats Satan. He sends him away.[14] In the mechanics of empowerment then, Jesus has a story that indicates he met Satan and won, not by wielding the Spirit, but by safeguarding it from wrongful use. He is therefore a fitting guardian of the Spirit.

Starting actions

According to Mark, again, 'after John was arrested, Jesus went to Galilee, proclaiming God's good news (*euangelion*, 'gospel'), saying: "The time is up, the Kingdom of God is close; trust in the good news."'[15] There is huge urgency in this statement. It is a proclamation demanding change. But why would anyone have believed Jesus?

The mechanics of empowerment is not just about claiming visions or telling stories. Alternative power needs to be proven by actions. The Gospel of Mark proceeds to demonstrate how Jesus proved John the Baptist's prediction true: Jesus immerses people in Holy Spirit, by dunking (immersing) unclean spirits inside them in Holy Spirit. Calling for repentance and proclaiming the good news of the kingdom of God, like John, he rids people of troublesome demons sent by Satan to make human beings suffer. Such activity of demons was a widespread folk belief. In Mark, the Spirit, accompanied by Jesus' command, is like a light sabre that is able to penetrate into the inner being where these demons had taken hold, and purify someone from the inside out, expelling the evil spirits and thereby curing the afflicted person.[16] Jesus' healings are exorcisms: the pure Spirit, wielded by Jesus, removes the dirty demons time and again. People are freed. Repenting, their wrongdoings are forgiven and they – or those they love – are healed. The stories are replicated in other Gospels with additional examples.[17] As if time is short, Jesus even imparts power to representatives (the Twelve) to go out in his stead around Galilee, to drive out demons and proclaim the kingdom.[18]

In these stories Satan and all his minions in the human body do not stand a chance. The Gospel stories also present us with a clear message that a key part of the kingdom of God is human wellness: disease and all forms of ill health are not from God and need to be eradicated. What Jesus does here is not only directly attack the dark side, demonstrating the deep compassion he feels for those who suffer, but he proves by miraculous actions that he has the Spirit, and what he says has the divine authority of God. In the mechanics of empowerment, actions are done so that words can then be heard. Jesus becomes a sensation. Jesus becomes a sensation, which suggests that the extent of ill health all over the region was very great, and Jesus was concerned by it. Mark records that huge crowds followed him from all the region in and around Galilee, and the demons, leaving the afflicted, would shout out, 'You are God's son!'[19]

Creating a core team

Jesus was not alone though; before he does a single healing, he gathers a team of disciples (students). The initial members of this team seem to have already been John the Baptist's disciples, at least according to the Gospel of John (John 1.35-51). Among them, Jesus targets fishers who worked on the Sea of Galilee, not wealthy entrepreneurs, not the people with social clout (Mark 1.16-20). He goes for a "bottom up" approach. These disciples are not utterly down and out street beggars; they had their own fishing boats, houses and enough money to hire day labourers if needed, but Peter and Andrew, James and John – sons of Zebedee – are not socially elite. They became his core.

Jesus also needed a home base, and this was Peter's house in Capernaum, on the shores of the lake, the Sea of Galilee, some 48 km by road from Nazareth. We are told nothing of Peter's family, but he has a mother in law who is healed of a fever.[20] The numbers of Jesus' disciples grow quickly, made up of a group of both men and women he identifies as his brothers and sisters (*adelphoi*), with a common Father in God. Thus, the so-called "Lord's Prayer" begins with the address 'Our Father in Heaven'.[21] That sounds a bit patriarchal, but in fact it takes away human patriarchy: Jesus says, 'Don't call anyone on earth "father" because you have one Father in Heaven'.[22] "God's son", the prime teacher, by implication is also situated in a wider category of "God's sons and daughters" that is expanded to include those who follow him as disciples, either on the road or in the villages and towns he visits. Implicitly this breaks down the hierarchy of the individual patriarchal family (a daughter is not necessarily to be obedient to her own father?), and also public institutions and the nation. The synagogue, for example, could be led by someone named the "father of the synagogue".[23] The honorific title *pater patriae*, "Father of the Fatherland", was conferred on emperors.

As for Jesus' own family, and those of his disciples, he had left them in Nazareth, in going to live with Peter in Capernaum. When they visited him, he was remarkably blasé. While they stand outside, Jesus is inside with his disciples, and he says: 'Who are my mother and my brothers and sisters?' And looking at those sitting in a circle around him, he said: 'Here are my brothers and sisters. One who does the will of God is my mother and sister and brother.'[24]

Honouring 'father and mother' as required by the law apparently then involved an alternative interpretation.[25] Jesus appears to have espoused detachment from one's own physical family for the sake of the greater good of the kingdom: the Aramaic word he used for 'detach' is probably *sna*, which was translated into Greek as *misei* ('hate'), leading to a dubious translation into Greek about 'hating' your own father and mother and family members.[26] But there is a cluster of sayings that clearly indicate that becoming a disciple of Jesus led to familial conflict.[27] Jesus did not shy away from making huge demands of his disciples, and you could end up being evicted from your family.

This was not an era of individuals making their personal choices: your life was dictated by the expectations of your family. In the mechanics of empowerment though, the call of Jesus to discipleship demanded that you make a choice. This overturned a primary building block of social power and constraint. If families could not control family members, then neither could villages and towns, and this could move right up through the hierarchy.

However, Jesus' teachings on family do not imply neglect of dependants. A husband was supposed to maintain his wife. Jesus interpreted Moses' law on divorce as being given to men because of their hard-heartedness, but in terms of the way things were designed by God in the beginning, a husband and a wife were one flesh that could not be separated.[28] This implies that male disciples who were married still needed to remain married and maintain their wives, presumably along with other dependants.[29] How all this actually worked out is something our stories do not tell.

Building a community

From the core team of disciples a new network was established that operated according to Jesus' teaching: this was the *ekklesia*, the 'assembly' or 'community' of Jesus' disciples. This community was founded on Jewish scripture and law, but the law was enacted in accordance with Jesus' interpretations (as in the case of divorce), given with the guidance of the Spirit. It was a prefiguring of the kingdom of God, a 'best case' scenario that still had to operate within the rubric of the world being Satan's dominion. The ideal of the kingdom of

God, soon to arrive in totality, created a rationale for present behaviour.

The way Jesus' dream of a future world is described in the Gospels, the kingdom of God is an idea of the earth's restoration with humanity in its right place, behaving as we should, in a caring, communal, egalitarian way (as brothers and sisters). Unlike in Plato's *Republic*, Jesus is never recorded as spelling out in detail what it means to live in this type of world, though clearly it involved following the law according to his interpretations. The ideal he has of this different way of living and his specific teaching on ethical behaviour (e.g. in the 'Sermon on the Mount') functions as a further basis, as well as a direct critique of the behaviour of those who currently have earthly power and authority. Living in the community involved the antithesis of gaining riches, or engaging in the desires and worries of this world.[30]

In Mark, after commending a rich man for following Jewish law meticulously, Jesus asks him to 'go and sell everything you own and give the money to the poor . . . then come, follow me'. As the rich man appears disheartened at this, Jesus states that it is extremely hard for rich people 'to enter the kingdom of God'.[31] Entering the kingdom is not just for the future; it is here and now in the *ekklesia* community. Such actions of giving away all your possessions can only take place because the community exists. Jesus is not asking the rich man to give away everything to be destitute on the streets and alone; rather, *to follow* Jesus in joining the community in which everyone's needs will be satisfied, as a prequel to what the kingdom will be. The Gospels do not explain how this works, but in the Acts of the Apostles it is described precisely: no one claimed anything for their own use, goods were held in common, and if anyone owned land or houses they would sell them and bring them to the apostles (for redistribution).[32] It could not be clearer. To follow Jesus and be in the *ekklesia* of disciples implied a radical lifestyle of shared resources distributed according to need.

In terms of ethics, beyond what was already written in Jewish law, Jesus emphasized that among his disciples love, mercy and forgiveness are to be the priority: before you pray, forgive everyone; love God and your neighbour; don't look to gain prestige; don't criticize your brothers and sisters, but rather look to doing better yourself. Actions count. It's not about calling Jesus 'lord' that matters, but doing the will of God, acting on Jesus' words; this is building your house on rock.[33]

The kingdom is then a utopia that can already be established here and now in this present world, as a reality among Jesus' disciples, if they choose to follow his message. It is not just a case of waiting and seeing, but actively doing something: joining a community of disciples in which people are brothers and sisters together, living with shared resources in a relatively non-hierarchical system. The inferior in this world would be the superior in the kingdom, and vice versa, so you need to think where you stand. The kingdom of God starts small, like a seed that is planted, but can grow big.[34] The Roman Empire, like other kingdoms of this world, has grown by military might, under the tutelage of Satan. This is why Jesus' kingdom – the kingdom of God – is 'not of *this* world'.[35]

Speaking out

One of the problems of interpreting Jesus' teaching is to know when precisely he is speaking to his disciples to guide their actions within the *ekklesia* community, when he is talking to them in relation to outsiders, or when he is talking to outsiders alone. Jesus' teaching, as collected in Matthew's 'Sermon on the Mount', is prefaced as indicating he was speaking to the 'crowds'. It certainly begins that way with a proclamation about the coming kingdom in which people who are poor in spirit, gentle and mournful, who hunger and thirst for righteousness, and are merciful, pure in heart, peacemakers and persecuted for what is right and abused will be given relief,[36] but the substance of the teaching jumps from this proclamation to something that targets his group of disciples as the 'salt of the earth' and 'light of the world'.[37]

Jesus states, 'Don't judge, and you won't be judged,' but the saying is part of a larger one in which he states 'why do you look at the splinter in your brother/sister's eye and not notice the plank in your own?'[38] The teaching here then is designed for his disciples living in the community, who are 'brothers and sisters', with one Father, who should live together harmoniously. When it comes to outsiders though, especially those in power, Jesus is anything but uncritical or non-judgemental. He points out the splinters and the planks.

Jesus hit out at those with authority especially hard. Jesus directly challenged those who were held in esteem as legal experts: the elite scribes (religious authorities), members of legal schools (Pharisees, Sadducees, Herodians), chief priests and the rich in general. The scribes were pointed out as men who like to wear fancy clothes and get respectful greetings, sit in the front seats of synagogues and special places of honour at banquets, yet who 'devour widows' houses' while reciting prayers in a showy way.[39] Public broadcasting of your religious excellence was bad news (it played into a concern with worldly honour), and heartless actions invalidated this claim anyway. Jesus accused the Pharisees and scribes of being hypocrites, doing pious things for show, laying unfair burdens on people, concentrating on superficial things in the law and neglecting the weighty ones like justice, mercy and faith.[40]

Given these were the most respected men in the community, aiming for a high standard of religious excellence, Jesus did not mince his words and avoid conflict. Seeing injustices done to people by those with authority ('devour widows' houses'), he spoke out. They also hit at Jesus, accusing him of transgressing the Sabbath law that no work should be done.[41] You can imagine why the authorities were concerned. As a Sabbath transgressor, how could Jesus' healings be powered by the Holy Spirit, because how could God be on the side of a Sabbath-transgressor? Scribes, who came to Galilee from the legal centre of Jerusalem, pronounced that Jesus cast out demons by the prince of demons, Beelzebub.[42] This would make Jesus into a sorcerer, a crime deserving the death penalty.[43] Perhaps for this reason, Jesus claimed that this insult to the Holy Spirit would 'never be forgiven'.[44]

Aligning God and nature

Jesus' basis for speaking out, as the empowered agent of God, rested on a received worldview that divides the human world into two parts: on the one side there is God and on the other side there is Satan. On the one side there are God's pure angels that provide protection and health, and on the other there are Satan's demons, the unclean spirits, which cause illness. In the Dead Sea Scrolls and in other Jewish literature of this period, the world is seen as highly dualistic, in that there is a battle between good and evil, light and darkness, truth and falsehood. The human world is fundamentally under the dominion of Satan.

In the Gospel of John, Satan is called the 'prince of this world'.[45] But we need to be careful when we read the word 'world' (*kosmos*) here: 'this world' is not the earth pitted against a rarefied heavenly realm. It is not that matter is inherently bad and will end totally, to be replaced by a spiritual reality. Stoic philosophers of the Graeco-Roman world had a scientific theory in which the universe turns in cycles of creation and destruction, the latter called the *ekpyrosis*, or 'conflagration', in which the material world would be entirely burnt up and then restored. The apostle Paul appealed to these Stoic ideas in his own "end of the world" scenario, in which there is a conflagration, though in this Christians would be re-clothed with an imperishable, spiritual body and float upwards to heaven like angels.[46] Paul even said that 'flesh and blood cannot inherit the Kingdom of God'.[47] But we have to be careful not to read these comments, perhaps strategically designed for a non-Jewish audience, into Jesus.

For Jesus, his teaching indicates that the earth itself, the natural world, is actually just as it should be. Nature is in the hands of God, and operates according to God's design and care. Jesus looks to nature in his parables to understand what the kingdom of God is about: God feeds birds and clothes flowers, and thus nature communicates God's message.[48] God does not use nature to punish anyone: God has the sun come up and sends rain on good and bad alike, and accidents happen without God punishing anyone either.[49] Nature is there to sustain humans, but God is aligned with continual processes of creation and destruction, benefits and hazards to humans included, within the cycles of nature.

Nature will be affected in the transformation of the world, when the kingdom comes in totality. As when there are burning fires, 'the sun will darken' and 'the moon will lose its brightness', or, as in the case of a meteor shower, 'stars will come falling from heaven' and 'the powers in the heavens will be shaken'. As with good natural processes like rain and sunrises, natural disasters are difficult for everyone, but are not meted out against the unjust only for specific punishment.[50]

Jesus uses the language of earthquakes and catastrophes to imagine the transformation, as nature participates in the transformation with 'birthpangs'.[51] The 'sky and the earth' will 'pass by', or 'move on' (*pareleusontai*),[52] that is change, but Jesus' words will not.[53] In the mechanics of empowerment this demonstrates God's close alignment with the natural world as God's domain. Jesus did not just have God on his side; he had all of nature as well: sky (heaven) and earth.

In Jesus' "nature miracles" then, the natural world does the bidding of the Spirit/God. Jesus can calm down a storm, make more food to feed people gathered in community to hear him, or make water take his weight and walk on it.[54] In the Gospel of John, these are understood as "signs": he can effectively make new eyes for a man born blind.[55] Such stories indicate where Jesus can act, as God's agent, with enormous power.

Human bodies, also, where Satan has taken hold, can be acted on and purified, once human will turns to repentance. But the human will itself is outside Jesus' control. Jesus, as God's agent, cannot zap people into awareness by any mind control. Human decisions are made by free choice, and Satan, with massive lures at his disposal, is winning.

Divorcing God from human authority

The problem with the world is that, unlike nature, the human world has become alienated from God, and God does not rule. The mythological foundation for this is found in the ancient legend of Adam and Eve and their establishment in the primeval Garden of Eden as its caretakers, yet with free will.[56] Choosing to disobey God's instructions, they ate of the tree of the knowledge of good and evil, and understood (unlike the animals) morality, only to bring disaster upon themselves:

they were cast out of the garden where all their food was provided and had to grow it themselves, women had to bear children in pain and be subject to their husbands, snakes lost their legs and slithered on the ground, and so on. From then on, it is a story of hardship and alienation, with some good choices, and quite a lot of bad ones, as the story of humanity, and then Israel, is told through the book of Genesis. In the alienation from God, in Judaism of this era, Satan holds sway; in the return to God, there is implied hope for a return to the garden, to the life of Adam and Eve pre-error: humans living as caretakers of God's earth, yearning for nothing else. Jesus' message was, therefore, about this change, about proclaiming the good news ('gospel') of a better life of humans on earth: the kingdom of God.

There is nothing God can do about human decisions that end up with abuse. Jesus' teaching is pacifist in that he does not suggest striking back at people who strike you or resisting soldiers that demand you carry their baggage as they march down the road.[57] Paradoxically, he suggests his disciples offer the other cheek for another blow and go another mile with a heavy load. This might be a means of shocking the abusers into self-reflection, but, ultimately, you can be sure that whatever wrong is done to you will have "karmic" consequences, just as what you do will come back to you. If you are heartless and judge your brothers and sisters harshly, all this will be thrown back in your face; if you show mercy and compassion, likewise.[58] Jesus proclaims a fairly simple system of what you give out you will get back in return, but not in the here and now.

Judgement, which will take place ahead of the arrival of the full totality of the kingdom, is the simple consequence of your own judgements, given human free will. Judgement deals with the problem of people who have just not repented at the time the kingdom comes in full. At this point, according to Jesus, there will be no second chance. The Gospel of Matthew spells it all out in quite vivid terms. In the parable of the weeds, a farmer sows wheat but an enemy sows weeds in the field as well, and the two types of plants grow together. At harvest the weeds are gathered up and thrown on the fire. Angels will come and gather up from the kingdom 'all the impediments and all who do lawlessness, and they will throw them into the furnace of fire'.[59] It's not pretty. In Gehenna's fire people will be incinerated. Given two men in the field, one will be taken and one released; given two women grinding, one will be taken and one released.[60] To be taken is not a good thing. You are going on the fire – not a place of torture, but of obliteration, non-existence, where body and soul are burnt up, with wailing and gnashing of teeth.[61] In this image, though, those who will remain and be taken off are male field workers and women grinding wheat/barley, and both are examples of ordinary villagers, so it is not simply about class struggle. One's family members and companions could be alongside the systemic oppressors.

It seems repugnant that a good and loving God could also oversee the annihilation of anyone. But, in the mechanics of empowerment, given the cultural beliefs of the time, this ghastly dream of the future functioned as a powerful incentive. It provided a threat. Judgement was not Jesus' invention, and it was widely believed among Jews that such an event would occur. It is founded on the idea that God is morally just and does not let wrongdoing go in the end. Those who are heartless and benefit from Satan's dominion are not going to be living in the kingdom, and there is only so much time for their repentance and different choices. Up until the day of reckoning God would be endlessly forgiving whenever people repented of their ways. But then time runs out. People had to choose. Life or death?

This imminent threat created an urgency, a time sensitivity, to Jesus' message. Jesus apparently even proclaimed that there were people of his time who would see the kingdom come in its totality.[62] It was all about acting now before it was too late. If there was no urgency, or danger, after all, why would anyone change?

This image of obliteration also suggests that there was social anger and a hunger for retribution against oppressors and collaborators who had caused harm. People would not have imagined the burning up of wrongdoers unless they felt deeply aggrieved. Jesus could harness this anger. In the Gospel of Luke, when Jesus speaks at the synagogue in Nazareth, he uses the prophet Isaiah and states that he is going to 'bring good news to the poor, liberty to captives and release to prisoners':[63] this implies the poor have been downtrodden, and that captives/prisoners in the current legal system need releasing. It therefore indicates no faith whatsoever in the legal system. The legal system, managed and operated by the wealthy and powerful, in collaboration with the Roman Empire, could not bring about true justice. This dream of judgement is therefore the dream of the powerless and the injured: they are angry.

Jesus specifically states also in Luke that he stands with the poor, hungry, sad and socially condemned. He is not with the rich, well fed, laughing and socially prestigious.[64] If you benefit from the world's current system, then you are in the wrong, and 'woe to you', because judgement is coming.

Jesus never explicitly denounces the emperor or the Roman imperial system. He does not have to. Given the dualism of Jesus' worldview, all worldly power is essentially not on the side of God. He very cleverly sidesteps the question about whether one should pay taxes to 'Caesar' in Jerusalem: he asks to see a coin that has an image of the emperor, and notes the image. So, 'give to Caesar what is Caesar's and to God what is God's'. At one and the same time, he accepts payment of taxes to Rome, much as he accepts being struck on the cheek, but also defines Caesar and the monetary system as opposite to God. In a dualistic way of thinking, money/Caesar is on the Satan side.[65] The world, operating on a financial system of money with Caesar's image on it, is all part of Satan's dominion. Operations of trade and the business of acquiring wealth and goods are all dismissed: ultimately, for Jesus, 'you cannot serve God and mammon (money, material possessions)'.[66]

Dying

The story that unfolds in the Gospels is one in which a small seed is planted, and God's son is shown as having tremendous power, but the world is so much on Satan's side that God's son is put to death. This is not the high action victory drama of a superhero movie. It is far, far more complex and mysterious.

The story of Jesus is one of conflict with authority: just as John the Baptist is arrested, and then killed, the pattern continues with Jesus. Prophets, we are told, invariably get killed by the powerful.[67] So when Jesus sets his sights on going to Jerusalem with his disciples for the festival of Passover, he tells them he is about to die.[68] As Jesus in the Gospel of John has it, with a nature allegory: 'Unless a grain of wheat falls to the ground and dies it stays alone, but if it dies it brings produce.'[69]

When Jesus arrives in Jerusalem, he does the opposite of keeping his head down, given that he has already been criticized for not observing the Sabbath correctly and using Beelzebub to cure people in order to lead them astray. He goes into the Temple and creates a disturbance, knocking over the tables where money changers were sitting to provide the

Temple currency for buying sacrifices and making donations. Jesus claims that the place that should be the 'house of prayer for all nations' has been turned into 'a cave of brigands'. The house of God itself had been corrupted. This statement has been interpreted in many ways by commentators, and some believe it indicates that Jesus denounced the whole sacrificial cult system. But really in Mark 11:15-19 the dualistic contrast is between the '*cave* of brigands' (i.e. sellers *and buyers*, money-changers, pigeon-sellers, carriers of goods) and a '*house of prayer* for all nations'. Trade in the Temple involved Satan sitting in the holiest place on earth. The very stones were violated. There was something very wrong, and Jesus predicted that the Temple would be destroyed.[70]

Such inflammatory actions and statements by Jesus combined with widespread popularity must have put the High Priest, Caiaphas, in a difficult position. Appointed by the Romans, he was as much a client ruler as Antipas was. His rule was not just over the Temple operations, but rather over the entire Judaean legal system and national functions, with significant responsibility also for Jews living abroad. He had to balance operations of jurisdiction, national administration and religion with deferring to the Roman military administration, based in Caesarea, on matters of security and taxation.

Caiaphas could make decisions unilaterally as a ruler, at any time, without seeking advice from a court, though he had a council of advisors. Acting against Jesus (as Sabbath breaker, magician and Temple defamer), however, might have sparked widespread public hostility, since he was being hailed as a prophet. With Jesus also being proclaimed as 'God's son' and Messiah/Christ – a king of the Judaeans – there were even more serious issues. Only Rome had the right to appoint client rulers. There was no national autonomy in the Empire.

Any self-proclaimed king was, by definition, acting against the emperor, and that was treason/sacrilege, thus a matter for the Roman military administration: the prefect Pontius Pilate. Therefore, regardless of what had been decided by the scribes about Jesus' idiosyncratic, self-authorized legal interpretations and charismatic programme of healing, the most pressing problem was what his claim to be king meant to the Romans. Caiaphas had to let the Romans deal with Jesus, if he was to be a loyal client ruler of Rome, and keep the peace. In the way the Gospels tell the story, the Judaean authorities are utterly compromised. The Gospel of John has the High Priest and his associates affirm to Pilate: 'We have no king but Caesar' (John 19.15).

As for Jesus, he must have known that he could not expect to proclaim his message in Satan's dominions and live. The Spirit gave him power over unclean demons, and worked wonders with God's natural world, but in terms of human will, and human authorities, Jesus – and his disciples – could only submit when faced with physical, hegemonic might. What happens though is an extraordinary paradox. In the Gospel of Mark, Jesus states he is indeed Christ (King) and God's son not in front of the crowds who adore him in Galilee but in the High Priest's house, after he had been arrested and interrogated.[71] Jesus is now at his most vulnerable, not at his most glorious. He is one of the prisoners he had announced he would free; he is one subject to the legal system wielded by those who had gained worldly power, and in response to his announcement of kingship, he is spat on, mocked and beaten. The reaction is that he deserves death, for "blasphemy", and it might be read that this is against God; but here the irony is that it is really against the emperor. For this reason, the High Priest and his council of advisors send Jesus to Pilate for his decision; they do not condemn Jesus to stoning.[72]

The paradox plays out as Pilate, the emperor's man, does as expected in Satan's dominion, and sends to his death the true Son of God, executed for treason, with all that entailed. The sign that told of his crime said: 'King of the Judaeans'. Hung next to a tortured and dying man, the mockery is obvious. You would think Satan had won, but in the Gospel of Mark things already start cracking the moment Jesus dies, when a Roman centurion, seeing this, states, 'Surely this man is God's son'.[73] In dying, Jesus' message goes straight to Rome, right there at the cross, in the seed planted in the centurion's mind on seeing the death of a martyr. Satan might have thought he had won, but Jesus' death, more than anything, takes the message out. We don't even have to read the resurrection accounts to know what Jesus' death was going to do.

Summing up

How do I see Jesus? I see him as a Jewish man of long ago who was courageous, compassionate, full of spiritual knowledge, radical, fiercely critical of the rich and powerful, and determined to change the world. So indeed he was a revolutionary, as well as a prophet. He was known as someone who could channel spiritual power, but his concerns were with the here and now, and with the powerless. He was a visionary, a dreamer and a spiritually gifted person with a special connection to God.

As for 2000 years later: what would Jesus do?

Since Jesus died criticizing those in power and proclaiming that God was with the downtrodden in a heartless world driven by the desire for power, status and wealth, he definitely took sides. Not only did he actively seek to alleviate suffering by his healing mission and align himself with nature, he created a community of people living according to different economics than the world around: sharing resources, caring for each other as egalitarian brothers and sisters, resisting the usual building blocks of hierarchical power structures, from family to village to city to nation. Jesus and his disciples did not choose to obey worldly power, even if they had to submit to it, because they answered to an alternative power that was greater than Caesar.

On the wall of the protesters in London in 2011, there was a sign that stated: 'The beginning is nigh.' I think Jesus would have agreed with that. The problem though is how to translate what Jesus called for in his own time into a reality that fits with today's meanings. I wonder what the consequences would be.

Notes

Jesus and the mechanics of empowerment

1 Matt. 21.12-17; Mark 11.15-19; Luke 19.45-48, cf. John 2.13-16.
2 The technical term for this is 'unitarian', as opposed to a 'trinitarian' who sees Jesus as equally human and divine, the second person in a divine trinity of God the Father, God the Son and God the Holy Spirit.
3 Josephus, *War* 2.68; *Ant.* 18.27.
4 Jerusalem: Josephus, *War* 2.409; Caesarea: Josephus, *War* 1.414.
5 Philo, *Legatio ad Gaium* 299-305.
6 Treason (*maiestas*) was linked with sacrilege. Suetonius (*Caligula* 27) records ghastly punishments for refusal to swear by the spirit *genius* of the Emperor Caligula; and see too, for example, Tacitus, *Hist.* 2:50; *Annals* 6:47.

7 God's son: Psalm 2.7; Dead Sea Scrolls 4Q174, 4Q246; the beloved one: Neh. 13.26; Ps. 45.1, 60.5; 108.6.

8 The Aramaic and Hebrew word for the sky and heaven is the same: *shemayin/shemayim.*

9 Wisdom of Solomon 7.22-27.

10 The Aramaic/Syriac it is *ruḥa d-qudsha,* Spirit of Holiness, or *ruḥa qadishta,* 'Holy Spirit'. In the early Syriac-speaking church, this feminine gender is used metaphorically to develop imagery of the mothering Spirit, and see Jerome, *Commentary on Isaiah* 40. 9-11; *The Testimony of Truth* 39. 26-30; *Gospel of Thomas* 101; *Gospel of Philip* 55. 23-26; 71. 3-16. In Greek the Holy Spirit is *to pneuma to hagion* (neuter) and in Latin *spiritus sanctus* (masculine) and the feminine associations are lost.

11 Mark 1.12-13.

12 Mark 14.32-42, and see Heb. 5.7.

13 Matt. 4.8-9.

14 Matt. 3.10.

15 Mark 1.15-16.

16 Mark 1.23-28; 1.29-31; 1.40-45; 2.1-12; 3.1-6; 3.22; 5.1-20; 5.21-24; 5.25-34; 7.24-30, 7.31-36; 8.22-26; 9.14-29; 10. 46-52.

17 Matt. 8.5-13; Luke 7.1-10; John 4. 46-54; Luke 7.11-17; Luke 22.50-51 cf. John 18.26; Luke 13.10-17; 14.1-6; 17.11-19; John 5.1-9; 9; 11.

18 Mark 3.14; 6:7.

19 Mark 3.7-12.

20 Mark 1.29-31.

21 Matt. 6.9.

22 Matt. 23.9.

23 CIJ 1.533; CIJ 1.508; JIWE 2.544; CIJ 1. 109; JIWE 2.93; CIJ 1.508; JIWE 2.544. The term 'mother of the synagogue' is also found: JIWE 1.5; 2.251, 542, 577.

24 Mark 3.32-35 and see Matt. 12.47-50; Luke 8.20-21; Gospel of Thomas 99. Nowhere else is a disciple of Jesus as such called a 'mother'. In Aramaic and Hebrew this can be a respectful term for an older woman. In Mark 5:34 Jesus curiously calls a woman stricken with a period lasting 12 years 'daughter' (in Aramaic *berat*), which can be a respectful term for 'girl'.

25 Exod. 20:12, and see Matt. 10.37.

26 Luke 14.25-27; Gospel of Thomas 55, 101

27 Mark 10.29-30, and see Luke 18.29; Matt. 10.37. Tellingly: 'Do not suppose that I have come to bring peace to the earth. It is not peace I have come to bring but a sword. For I have come to set son against father, daughter against mother, daughter in law against mother in law. A person's enemies will be the members of their own household', Matt. 10.34-36; Luke 12.51-53 adds "mother against daughter".

28 Mark 10.2-12, and see Matt. 19.3-10; Matt. 5.31-32; Luke 16.18; Matthew 8.18-22; Luke 14.25-27; Matthew 10.21-22.

29 Understandably, perhaps, the male disciples respond by saying that if this is so it is better not to marry (Matt. 19:10).

30 Mark 4.18-19.

31 Mark 10.17-27.

32 Acts 4.32, 34-35.

33 Mark 11.25; 12.28-34; 38-40; Matt. 7.1-5; 21-27.

34 Mark 4.1-34.

35 John 18.36.

36 Matt. 5.3-12.

37 Matt. 5.13-16.

38 Matt. 7.1-5.

39 Mark 13.38-40.

40 Matt. 23.

41 Exod. 20.8-11 also 35:2; Mark 2.23-3.6.

42 Mark 3.22-27.

43 Deut. 18.10-11; Mishnah, Sanhedrin 7.7.

44 Mark 3.28-30.

45 John 12.31; 14.30

46 1 Cor. 15.20-28, 50-57; 2 Cor. 5.1-10; 1 Thess. 4.13-5.10;
   2 Thess. 1.6-2.12; Col. 3.1-4; Phil. 1.18-28

47 1 Cor. 15.50.

48 Mark 4. 26-32; 13. 30; Matt. 6.25-33

49 Matt. 5.45; Luke 13.2-5.

50 Matt. 24.19.

51 Matt. 24.7-8

52 Often this is translated as 'will pass away' as if everything
   will be destroyed, but this is not quite correct. The word
   is repeated over verses 30 and 31: 'this generation will
   not move/pass on before all these things will have taken
   place; the sky and the earth will move/pass on but my
   words will not move/pass on.' There is progression but not
   destruction.

53 Mark 13.24-27, 31.

54 Mark 4.35-41; 6.30-52; 9.1-10.

55 John 9.

56 Genesis 1-3.

57 Matt. 5.38-42.

58 Matt. 7.1; Luke 6.37.

59 Matt. 13.24-30, 36-43.

60 Matt. 24.37-41.

61 Matt. 10.28.

62 Mark 13.30.

63 Isa. 61.1; Luke 4.18.

64 Luke 6.20-26.

65 Mark 12.13-17.

66 Matt. 6.24.

67 Luke 6.23.

68 Mark 8.30-33; 9.30-32.

69 John 12.24.

70 Matt. 24.1; Mark 13.1-2; Luke 21.5-6.
71 Mark 14.60-61,
72 The death penalty for blasphemy against God was within the jurisdiction of the High Priest; thus Stephen is stoned to death in Acts 7.
73 Mark 15.39.

Was Jesus an ethical revolutionary?[1]

ROBIN GILL

You may think that the obvious answer to this question is simply 'yes'. Whether you believe that Jesus was the Son of God or just a very unusual gifted human being, you might agree that Jesus had a distinctive ethical message that has had a major impact upon Western, and even some non-Western, thought. Tolstoy, as a free-thinking Christian novelist, and Gandhi, as a Hindu political activist, alike, reached this conclusion, as have many other influential thinkers and writers. Religious and secular humanists have often concluded that, whatever their disagreements about the existence of God or afterlife, the ethical teaching of Jesus *was* indeed revolutionary.

In the first half of this article I will try to persuade you that the answer might reasonably be 'no'. Only in the second half will I offer my own very specific 'yes'.

However, before launching out, a number of crucial decisions need to be taken. Like the Buddha and Socrates, Jesus left no writing of his own. His words are always mediated through others, most (if not all) who wrote long after his death. In the New Testament, Paul wrote earlier than others, but he never met Jesus during his lifetime and showed more interest in his theological significance than in his ethical teaching. Modern New Testament scholars consider Mark to be the earliest of the Gospels, but date it to a good generation after the death of Jesus. They also agree that Matthew and Luke knew and used Mark (and were, therefore, later still) and most consider John to have been written some two of three generations after Jesus' death.

So, how do we establish what Jesus' ethical teaching really was?

For more than a century, scholars have debated this question, with some convinced that it is possible to piece together the 'authentic' teaching of Jesus but others not. This is very slippery territory, and I am not an enthusiastic skater. Instead, I will mainly confine my discussion to the ethical teaching of Jesus as variously presented in the different Gospels, without making too many claims about whether or not it is possible to dig behind them, let alone behind their written or oral sources. It is, after all, these Gospels, as they stand, that have influenced Western thought.

However, in doing so, I have already made another decision, namely that the Gospels may themselves differ in their presentations of the ethical teaching of Jesus. It has long been recognized that John is very different from the other three. Today, though, most scholars recognize that Matthew and Luke have some crucial ethical differences in the way that they use Mark.

The following two examples of unusually explicit ethical teaching show this clearly:

In Mark, as Jesus was setting out on a journey, a man ran up and knelt before him, and asked him, 'Good Teacher, what must I do to inherit eternal life?' (Mark 10.17). After some discussion Jesus concluded: 'You lack one thing; go, sell what you own, and give (the money) to the poor, and you will have treasure in heaven; then come, follow me'. Matthew follows Mark quite closely here, but Luke significantly adds an extra word to Jesus' conclusion: 'sell *all* that you own and distribute (the money) to the poor' (Luke 18.22). Indeed, at several points Luke is more emphatic than either Mark or Matthew about the evils of wealth and the virtues of poverty and, here at least, makes a near impossible demand. . . a bit like the ironic command to 'let the dead bury their own dead' (Luke 9.60).

In Mark again, Jesus was asked about whether he considered divorce to be lawful. After some discussion, he concluded without qualification that, 'Whoever divorces his wife and marries another commits adultery against her; and if she divorces her husband and marries another, she commits adultery' (Mark 10.11-12). Matthew includes this story (Luke does not) but modifies the conclusion to, 'whoever divorces his wife, except for unchastity, and marries another commits adultery' (Matthew 19.9). This is another very significant difference (albeit with Mark here being the most uncompromising) – a difference that has divided Christians in the modern world and led to very different church policies on marriage after divorce.

Pitfalls abound here. Even the very concept of 'ethics' is not straightforward. In the West today it has been shaped variously by giants such as Thomas Aquinas, David Hume and Immanuel Kant. Of these three only Aquinas paid careful attention to the New Testament, and even he had some quirky (to modern minds) takes on it. He concluded, for example, that Jesus' command to Peter at Gethsemane to 'put your sword back into its sheath' (John 18.11) meant, among other things, that clergy should not take part in jousting.

1. Jesus *was not* a revolutionary

Whatever the pitfalls, it is possible to suggest some decidedly non-revolutionary features of the ethical teaching of Jesus as variously presented in Mark, Matthew and Luke.

Pragmatism

Despite his principled passion against wealth, Luke does have some surprisingly pragmatic touches. For example, he alone has this parable of Jesus:

> What king, going out to wage war against another king, will not sit down first and consider whether he is able with ten thousand to oppose the one who comes against him with twenty thousand? If he cannot, then, while the other is still far away, he sends a delegation and asks for the terms of peace (Luke 14.31-32).

Admittedly Luke gives this parable (in a somewhat convoluted way) his characteristic explanation: 'So therefore, none of you can become my disciple if you do not give up all your possessions'. Yet it does suggest (again to modern minds) an unexpected level of pragmatism.

This suspicion is reinforced by awareness that the 'probability of success' was formally added later to so-called just-war theory. Unsurprisingly, the very notion of a 'just war' is not present in the New Testament at all. Within Christianity Bishop Ambrose and then Augustine first developed it in the fourth century from classical sources, and only once Christianity had been adopted as a state religion. At this stage the notions of a 'just authority' and 'just intention' were crucial. Over time just causes for going to war (*ius ad bellum*) have usually been extended to seven criteria: just cause; competent authority;

comparative justice; right intention; last resort; probability of success; and proportionality. In addition, just practices within war (*ius in bello*) have been assessed particularly in terms of proportionality and discrimination. Most recently, just war theorists have also developed criteria for just policies after war (*ius post bellum*). This whole area within military ethics now involves philosophers, politicians, lawyers and military strategists, who may or may not be aware of its theological roots (which are considerable).

Even more curious is the pragmatism that seems to be present in two of the elusive parables in Luke – that of the Unjust Manager and that of the Unjust Judge:

Jesus said to the disciples, 'There was a rich man who had a manager, and charges were brought to him that this man was squandering his property. So he summoned him and said to him, "What is this that I hear about you? Give me an account of your management, because you cannot be my manager any longer." Then the manager said to himself, "What will I do, now that my master is taking the position away from me? I am not strong enough to dig, and I am ashamed to beg. I have decided what to do so that, when I am dismissed as manager, people may welcome me into their homes." So, summoning his master's debtors one by one, he asked the first, "How much do you owe my master?" He answered, "A hundred jugs of olive oil." He said to him, "Take your bill, sit down quickly, and make it fifty." Then he asked another, "And how much do you owe?" He replied, "A hundred containers of wheat." He said to him, "Take your bill and make it eighty." And his master commended the dishonest manager because he had acted shrewdly; for the children of this age are more shrewd in dealing with their own generation than are the children of light. And I tell you, make friends for yourselves by means of dishonest wealth so that when it is gone, they may welcome you into the eternal homes. (Luke 16.1-9)

Jesus told them a parable about their need to pray always and not to lose heart. He said:

In a certain city there was a judge who neither feared God nor had respect for people. In that city there was a widow who kept coming to him and saying, "Grant me justice against my opponent." For a while he refused; but later he said to himself, "Though I have no fear of God and no respect for anyone, yet because this widow keeps bothering me, I will grant her justice, so that she may not wear me out by continually coming." ' And the Lord said, 'Listen to what the unjust judge says. And will not God grant justice to his chosen ones who cry to him day and night? Will he delay long in helping them? I tell you, he will quickly grant justice to them. And yet, when the Son of Man comes, will he find faith on earth? (Luke 18.1-8)

All sorts of ingenious theories have been offered to explain why either the manager or the judge was not in reality acting unethically. But, as they stand in Luke's Gospel, the manager *is* identified as 'dishonest' and the judge as 'unjust'. And the commendation to 'make friends for yourselves by means of dishonest wealth' appears woefully pragmatic, as does the judge's excuse that 'I will grant her justice, so that she may not wear me out by continually coming'.

Of course Luke's intentions here may have been deliberately ironic. There is a respected scholarly opinion that irony is a strong feature of Mark's Gospel too. Yet, whatever the intention, it is difficult to argue that any of these three parables in Luke support the contention that Jesus was an ethical revolutionary. An ironic, ethical commentator, perhaps, but not a revolutionary.

Nor do the confusing statements about divorce or wealth, already noted, support the contention that Jesus (as portrayed variously in the Gospels) was an ethical revolutionary.

Reward and Punishment

Another piece of evidence that pushes in a similar direction is that several of the parables appear to suggest that good actions will be rewarded in heaven and that bad actions will be punished in hell. There is a hint of this, perhaps, in the final two words of the parable of the unjust manager. However, it is particularly strong in one of the parables that Matthew alone tells – that of the Sheep and the Goats:

> When the Son of Man comes in his glory, and all the angels with him, then he will sit on the throne of his glory. All the nations will be gathered before him, and he will separate people one from another as a shepherd separates the sheep from the goats, and he will put the sheep at his right hand and the goats at the left. Then the king will say to those at his right hand, "Come, you that are blessed by my Father, inherit the kingdom prepared for you from the foundation of the world; for I was hungry and you gave me food, I was thirsty and you gave me something to drink, I was a stranger and you welcomed me, I was naked and you gave me clothing, I was sick and you took care of me, I was in prison and you visited me." Then the righteous will answer him, "Lord, when was it that we saw you hungry and gave you food, or thirsty and gave you something to drink? And when

was it that we saw you a stranger and welcomed you, or naked and gave you clothing? And when was it that we saw you sick or in prison and visited you?" And the king will answer them, "Truly I tell you, just as you did it to one of the least of these who are members of my family, you did it to me." Then he will say to those at his left hand, "You that are accursed, depart from me into the eternal fire prepared for the devil and his angels; for I was hungry and you gave me no food, I was thirsty and you gave me nothing to drink, I was a stranger and you did not welcome me, naked and you did not give me clothing, sick and in prison and you did not visit me." Then they also will answer, "Lord, when was it that we saw you hungry or thirsty or a stranger or naked or sick or in prison, and did not take care of you?" Then he will answer them, "Truly I tell you, just as you did not do it to one of the least of these, you did not do it to me." And these will go away into eternal punishment, but the righteous into eternal life. (Matthew 25.31-46)

This much-loved parable is particularly interesting for an ethicist because it seems to commend unselfconscious, altruistic action. The sheep are acting so virtuously that they are unaware that they had been caring for the Lord. Virtue ethicists call this *habitus*. Virtues have been so ingrained into the character of individuals that they are not even aware that this is so. These individuals simply *are* virtuous.

Yet, taken at face value, this interpretation is vitiated by the opening and closing statements. The virtuous sheep are told that they will 'inherit the kingdom prepared for you from the foundation of the world', whereas the goats, who lack virtues, are warned that they 'will go away into eternal punishment'.

Such a crude ethical basis is unlikely to commend itself to the modern world as the words of an ethical revolutionary. They appear more akin to the frequent denunciations of the Hebrew prophets.

2. Jesus *was* a revolutionary

Perhaps it is not surprising that conventional elements of ethical pragmatism, punishment and reward can be found in the Gospels. They are not remotely works of consistent moral philosophy. They have none of the uniform (some say 'over-uniform') principles that characterize the writings of, say Aquinas or Kant. Most critical scholars today conclude that Mark, and then Matthew and Luke, drew their material from a variety of sources while, at the same time, adding their own different slants to that material. So consistency is not to be expected. There are tensions within each of these Gospels as well as tensions between them.

However, there are some important strands that suggest that Jesus really was an ethical revolutionary. Three of these strands are particularly significant: The Golden Rule, The Neighbour-Love Command and, above all, the Enemy-Love Command. Each of these requires a high level of ethical altruism from the followers of Jesus. The first two have parallels in other religious faiths, but the third is more distinctively related to Jesus.

The Golden Rule in the Gospels

The Golden rule is explicit within both Matthew's 'Sermon on the Mount' and Luke's 'Sermon on the Plain'. Here Jesus commands:

In everything do to others as you would have them do to you; for this is the law and the prophets (Matthew 7.12).

Do to others as you would have them do to you (Luke 6.31).

It will be noticed that in Matthew's version Jesus is not claiming that this teaching is unique to himself. On the contrary, he sees it as part of the Jewish Law (i.e. the first five books of the Old Testament/Hebrew Bible/Tanakh, which are normative for Orthodox Jews) and of the later Prophets. In Matthew it is a summary of existing teaching.

Indeed, Rabbi Hillel, an approximate contemporary of Jesus, concluded from Leviticus 19.18 ('You shall not take vengeance or bear a grudge against any of your people, but you shall love your neighbour as yourself') that, 'What is hateful to you, do not do to your fellow: this is the whole Torah; the rest is the explanation; go and learn'.

The radical Catholic theologian Hans Küng has argued that similar versions of the Golden Rule can also be found in at least the following religious faiths:

> Confucius: 'What you yourself do not want, do not do to another person.'
> Islam: 'None of you is a believer as long as he does not wish his brother what he wishes himself.'
> Jainism: 'Human beings should be indifferent to worldly things and treat all creatures in the world as they would want to be treated themselves.'
> Buddhism: 'A state which is not pleasant or enjoyable for me will also not be so for him; and how can I impose on another a state which is not pleasant or enjoyable for me?'
> Hinduism: 'One should not behave towards others in a way which is unpleasant for oneself: that is the essence of morality.'[2]

However other theologians make a sharp distinction between negative versions of the Golden Rule (sometimes dubbed the

Silver Rule) and the two positive versions in Matthew and Luke (and, seemingly, Jainism as well).

Does this matter? Well it might. A negative version would surely conclude that most people (unless they were masochists) would not want to be tortured, so, according to the Silver Rule, they should not torture others. In contrast, the Golden Rule might emphasise positively that we should be kind to others, just as we would want others to be kind to us. Manifestly torturing someone is not being kind but being kind involves very much more than not torturing them. Some illustrate this difference by comparing negative human rights with positive human rights – the latter are usually considered to be much more demanding than the former.

Whether you agree with this argument or not, the Golden Rule is an important expression of ethical altruism; it is a feature of Jesus' teaching in Matthew and Luke, and it has become today an important feature of inter-faith dialogue. However, it is not unique to the ethical teaching of Jesus.

The Love Command in the Gospels

Some theologians claim that the double commands to love God and to love neighbour are unique to Jesus. This is the way it appears in the earliest Gospel:

> One of the scribes came near and heard them disputing with one another, and seeing that he answered them well, he asked him, 'Which commandment is the first of all?' Jesus answered, 'The first is, "Hear, O Israel: the Lord our God, the Lord is one; you shall love the Lord your God with all your heart, and with all your soul, and with all your mind, and with all your strength." The second is this, "You shall love your neighbour as yourself."

There is no other commandment greater than these'
(Mark 12.28-31).

Here Jesus – they argue – uniquely brought together the Shema
known to all pious Jews and recited by them morning and
evening every day. 'You shall love the Lord your God with all your
heart, and with all your soul, and with all your might (Deuteronomy 6.5) and a more obscure text, 'You shall not take vengeance
or bear a grudge against any of your people, but you shall love
your neighbour as yourself' (Leviticus 19.18). In addition, Jesus
uniquely expanded neighbour-love well beyond kin and immediate neighbours to *all* people and used a strong verb for 'love' for
both love of God *and* love of neighbour (in Greek *agapaö* rather
than *phileö*). This, it is claimed, is indeed revolutionary.

Unfortunately the first of these claims does not entirely stand
up to scrutiny. Despite knowing Mark, Luke offers a somewhat
different account of the same story:

Just then a lawyer stood up to test Jesus. 'Teacher,' he said,
'what must I do to inherit eternal life?' He said to him,
'What is written in the law? What do you read there?' He
answered, 'You shall love the Lord your God with all your
heart, and with all your soul, and with all your strength, and
with all your mind; and your neighbour as yourself.' And
he said to him, 'You have given the right answer; do this,
and you will live.' (Luke 10.25-28).

In this version, then, it is not Jesus who combines these two
commands from the Old Testament; it is the lawyer who does.
It also seems that, once again, there are contemporary examples
of other Jewish writers making a similar combination.

What about the claim that Jesus uniquely expands the term
'neighbour' here? Luke does seem to support this. Immediately

after this passage, in response to the lawyer's question 'And who is my neighbour?' Jesus gives the parable of the Good Samaritan. In this parable the Samaritan – a traditional enemy of the Jewish people – is the one who acts altruistically to the stranger unlike the two Jewish officials who 'pass by on the other side'. And, after the parable, Luke records Jesus saying:

> Which of these three, do you think, was a neighbour to the man who fell into the hands of the robbers?' He (i.e. the lawyer) said, 'The one who showed him mercy.' Jesus said to him, 'Go and do likewise.' (Luke 10.36-37).

This could indeed be revolutionary. It might even be Enemy-Love.

Enemy-Love in the Gospels

Matthew's 'Sermon on the Mount' and Luke's 'Sermon on the Plain' both put particular emphasis upon Jesus' teaching about Enemy-Love, as these remarkable passages both show:

> You have heard that it was said, 'You shall love your neighbour and hate your enemy.' But I say to you, Love your enemies and pray for those who persecute you, so that you may be children of your Father in heaven; for he makes his sun rise on the evil and on the good, and sends rain on the righteous and on the unrighteous. For if you love those who love you, what reward do you have? Do not even the tax-collectors do the same? And if you greet only your brothers and sisters, what more are you doing than others? Do not even the Gentiles do the same? Be perfect, therefore, as your heavenly Father is perfect. (Matthew 5.43-48)

Love your enemies, do good to those who hate you, bless those who curse you, pray for those who abuse you. If anyone strikes you on the cheek, offer the other also; and from anyone who takes away your coat do not withhold even your shirt. Give to everyone who begs from you; and if anyone takes away your goods, do not ask for them again. Do to others as you would have them do to you. If you love those who love you, what credit is that to you? For even sinners love those who love them. If you do good to those who do good to you, what credit is that to you? For even sinners do the same. If you lend to those from whom you hope to receive, what credit is that to you? Even sinners lend to sinners, to receive as much again. But love your enemies, do good, and lend, expecting nothing in return. (Luke 6.27-35)

There is a slight puzzle with the opening of this passage from Matthew: there is no command to 'hate your enemy' in the Old Testament, although some of the Psalms get quite close to that. But, more importantly, there is no command there to 'love your enemies'. *That* command, at least, is radically different – even revolutionary. There is, of course, a hint about reward. Yet even that gives way to a counsel of ethical perfection. Followers of Jesus are given the heroic command to 'pray for those who persecute you'. This is a highly demanding ethic, a revolutionary ethic.

Similarly in the passage from Luke, followers of Jesus are commanded to 'bless those who curse you, pray for those who abuse you'. . . and, then, to turn the other cheek, to give away their clothes and to lend without expecting any return. This too is, surely, a counsel of ethical perfection.

This command to Enemy-Love, for once, is also found in Paul's Letter to the Romans, written much earlier than

Matthew or Luke (although not necessarily much earlier than the written source that some scholars believe lies behind such material that Matthew and Luke have in common but did not find in Mark):

> Bless those who persecute you; bless and do not curse them. Rejoice with those who rejoice, weep with those who weep. Live in harmony with one another; do not be haughty, but associate with the lowly; do not claim to be wiser than you are. Do not repay anyone evil for evil, but take thought for what is noble in the sight of all. If it is possible, so far as it depends on you, live peaceably with all. Beloved, never avenge yourselves, but leave room for the wrath of God; for it is written, 'Vengeance is mine, I will repay, says the Lord.' No, 'if your enemies are hungry, feed them; if they are thirsty, give them something to drink; for by doing this you will heap burning coals on their heads.' Do not be overcome by evil, but overcome evil with good. (Romans 12.14-21)

The vengeful features of this passage are less endearing than the passages from Matthew and Luke, but the commands to 'bless those who persecute you' and to give food and drink to enemies are very similar and, indeed, just as radical. Given that Paul was himself once a persecutor, they are commands that were, doubtless, deeply felt by him. He had by now joined the persecuted and, as a follower of Jesus, he was committed to his revolutionary ethical teaching about Enemy-Love. Given that Matthew and Luke (and their possible common source) and Paul all knew about, and took seriously, this unparalleled, sustained teaching about Enemy-Love, it seems likely that it really does go right back to Jesus himself.

On this evidence, Enemy-Love does appear to have been a distinctive feature of Jesus' revolutionary ethic.

At a very minimum this ethic has had radical implications for the proper treatment of prisoners of war. Many today expect democratic societies to refrain from torture, to provide prisoners of war with adequate sustenance and shelter, and to treat them with respect. Lapses are rightly shamed and exposed by vigilant journalists, and politicians typically go to great lengths to explain that what appears to be 'torture' (such as waterboarding) is not really torture at all or, if it is, that it is ethically justifiable only because of exceptional circumstances. Despite the obvious hypocrisy here, such procrastinations clearly show that the politicians involved are only too aware that the mistreatment of prisoners of war is, indeed, wrong.

At a much higher ethical level, the revolutionary Enemy-Love Command has inspired some extraordinary acts of ethical heroism. Gordon Wilson and Pope John Paul II provide striking examples, but there are many other examples of less famous individuals acting in very similar ways. A mark of ethical revolutionaries is, perhaps, that they can inspire others to follow their behaviour. In that respect Jesus *was* an ethical revolutionary.

In 1987 Gordon Wilson, together with his twenty-year-old daughter Marie, took part in a Remembrance Day service around the local war memorial in Enniskillen in Northern Ireland. The IRA detonated a bomb during the service that buried them both in the rubble, killing her and injuring him. In the BBC interview that followed this atrocity, Wilson, a lifelong Methodist, spoke astonishingly as follows:

She held my hand tightly, and gripped me as hard as she could. She said, 'Daddy, I love you very much'. Those were her exact words to me, and those were the last words I ever heard her say. . . But I bear no ill will. I bear no grudge. Dirty sort of talk is not going to bring her back to life. She was a great wee lassie. She loved her profession. She was a pet. She's dead. She's in heaven and we shall meet again. I will pray for these men tonight and every night.

For the next two decades of his life Gordon Wilson worked for peace and reconciliation, not vengeance, in Northern Ireland. Assessments of his political significance have varied (although Enniskillen itself is now widely recognized as a turning point in The Troubles), but many have acknowledged his deep ethical heroism.

Political and ecclesiastical assessments of Pope John Paul II, unsurprisingly, have also varied. Yet his reaction to a very serious assassination attack by Mehmet Ali Agca in 1981, using a high-powered Browning automatic, has also been much admired by Catholics and non-Catholics alike. In the operation that followed the attack, he received some six pints of blood and remained physically frail for the rest of his life. Yet subsequently he went as a priest to Agca's prison cell, he met Agca's mother, and he asked people to 'pray for my brother. . . whom I have sincerely forgiven'. Finally, he was instrumental in securing Agca an early reprieve.

In his Message for World Day of Peace on New Year's Day 2002 he wrote poignantly:

The failure to forgive, especially when it serves to prolong conflict, is extremely costly in terms of human development. Resources are used for weapons rather than for development, peace and justice. What sufferings are inflicted on humanity because of the failure to reconcile!

What delays in progress because of the failure to forgive! Peace is essential for development, but true peace is made possible only through forgiveness.[3]

At the heart of this message is a plea for a radically different ethical order – Jesus' revolutionary order of forgiveness and Enemy-Love.

Notes

Was Jesus an ethical revolutionary?

1 I explore many of the ideas here further in my *Moral Passion and Christian Ethics* (Cambridge: Cambridge University Press, 2017).

2 Hans Küng's use of the Golden Rule across different faith traditions can be found in his *Global Responsibility: In Search of a New World Ethic* (New York: Continuum, 1991) and *A Global Ethic for Global Politics and Economics* (London: SCM Press, 1997), pp 98–99.

3 Pope John Paul II's Message for World Day of Peace on New Year's Day 2002 can be found at: <http://w2.vatican.va /content/john-paul-ii/en/messages/peace/documents/hf_jp -ii_mes_20031216_xxxvii-world-day-for-peace.html>

Jesus the storyteller: The revolutionary power of parables

AMY-JILL LEVINE

Where is revolution to be found?

I want Jesus to be 'revolutionary' or at least 'radical' (the current preferred term among liberal Christians) in part because the label sounds good. I have spent over half a century studying him, and it is depressing to think that this figure who so fascinates me would be something other than revolutionary or radical. Jesus was a healer and exorcist, no doubt charismatic, a visionary, eschatologically oriented and convinced that he was divinely commissioned to prepare his people—that is, Jews—for the inbreaking of the kingdom of God. He gathered crowds, and because he did, in Jerusalem at Passover, Caiaphas found him a danger to the peace of the city, and Pilate crucified him. His followers would then proclaim him as raised from the dead. Less clear is whether these traits amount to 'revolutionary.'

The topic of Jesus the 'revolutionary' is compromised by the investments of those who answer the question. Anyone who addresses the question is stuck with defining the term, and in good academic fashion, we assess the subject in light of the definition that best works for us.

Revolutionary comes to mean, especially in sectors of the academy as well as the popular imagination, what 'we' want. In this setting, 'change' is good, and the status quo is dreadful (no subtlety here, even if via colonial mimicry the 'new' is a replication of the old, just with different players).

My students, most of them studying to be Christian ministers and religious educators, and almost all of them invested in counter-cultural expressions, with the 'culture' defined variously as late global capitalism, colonialism, heteronormativity and anything to do with Donald Trump, require Jesus to be a revolutionary. They need him for their own ideological agendas. One can hear John Lennon and Paul McCartney in the background, 'You say you want a revolution.' Alas, too often this approach ignores the well-taken next stanzas, 'But when you talk about destruction, don't you know that you can count me out.' The revolutionary Jesus sounds good, but the question of what this revolution does remains vague. If Revolution means 'you want money for people with minds that hate' or 'carrying pictures of chairman Mao', then this is not the Jesus I know.

When I ask them to describe the ways in which they see Jesus to be 'revolutionary', many of their initial responses reflect either no knowledge of his social setting or, worse, a sense of both Rome and Second Temple Jewish practice as models of toxicity (insert here contemporary social issues). They then presume that Jesus speaks directly to their issues by taking texts out of both literary and historical contexts, by imposing their own agendas on the text and otherwise by making Jesus into a blank screen on which they can project their concerns. They make him a revolutionary who comes to do away with Rome (empire, politics as usual, non-egalitarian systems) and/or Second Temple Jewish life (ritual purity, ethnic identification, particularity). The flip side of the revolutionary Jesus threatens, always, to demonize those who do not follow him. The scene in Monty Python's 'Life of Brian', where the question is asked, 'what have the Romans ever done for us?' should be requisite viewing for all those who see Jesus as a 'revolutionary'. The answer to the question, by the way, is sanitation, medicine, education, wine, public order, irrigation, roads, a freshwater system and public health, along with 'bring peace'.

This concern to portray Jesus as revolutionary is particularly acute among the students with low Christology. Since they dismiss ideas of incarnation and resurrection as superstitious balderdash, the only way they can justify their membership as card-carrying Christians is to portray him as a revolutionary and a radical in his own time. This 'revolutionary, radical Jesus' serves as an ostensibly non-theological way of speaking of Jesus as unique. However, the category of unique functions as a theological placeholder. In this configuration, Jesus is the 'one and only human being who cares' about social justice, ecology, women's rights, anti-imperial politics and so on. Ironically, investing Jesus with a unique vision grants him divine status. This approach also has the side effect of ignoring the fact that revolutionaries aren't single agents: revolutionaries require followers, and sometimes it is the followers rather than the figurehead who produce the revolution. The 'change in the world' effects are created by his followers, who take Jewish theological claims, filtered through developing Christology, into the Gentile world. Thus, claims of Jesus the revolutionary always risk marginalizing the contributions of those who worked with him, especially women.

After addressing the popular views of Jesus the revolutionary, this essay turns to a usually overlooked subject when it comes to revolutionary activities, the parables, which is where I see revolution, or something like it, occurring. It may well turn out that the story is mightier than the sword.

Political revolution?

The revolutionary Jesus takes several forms: the man of peace who rejects the violence of the Zealots; the anti-Roman agitator who sought to promote a different kingdom; the economic reformer who rejects (the stereotype of) money-obsessed Jewish culture; the biblical conservative who rejects what comes to be characterized as Pharisaic teaching; the universalist who overcomes Jewish particularism; the ethical genius who promotes the Golden Rule against the stereotype of the egoistical Jew who at best can offer the Silver Rule; the friend of the marginal and the outcast vs. the stereotypical Jewish purity fanatics; the institutional critic who stops the Temple's exploitation of the poor . . . Few of these configurations work particularly well from an historical perspective, and most risk bleeding over into anti-Jewish stereotypes

Regarding the several political takes, apologetics sometimes enter under the guise of history, where the revolution Jesus promotes is distinct from all the other movements of the period and where, again, Jesus speaks to contemporary political as well as theological desiderata. On the one hand, we have Jesus as the anti-Roman Zealot, a point demonstrated by his crucifixion. Mark 15.26 states that Pilate crucifies Jesus under the political charge of 'king of the Jews', and the other Gospels follow Mark (Matthew 27.37; Luke 23.38; John 19.19) with John 19.20 adding that the inscription was in Hebrew, Greek and Latin. The problem here is that Jesus was not a political agitator, and Rome did not find him personally to be a threat.

Jesus accepts the title 'son of David' (e.g., Matthew 9.27; 15.22; 20.30; 21.9) and so presents himself as a king, but his programme is eschatological more than it is political. His concern is less Rome, and perhaps not even Rome: his native Galilee is not occupied, and he appears more concerned with bringing his message to the Temple than to Pilate. His programme is in bringing about the messianic age, when not just Rome, but the cosmos changes. The proponents of the anti-Roman revolutionary Jesus need to address texts such as Mark 13.26–27: 'Then they will see "the Son of Man coming in clouds" with great power and glory. Then he will send out the angels, and gather his elect from the four winds, from the ends of the earth to the ends of heaven.' The term Parousia is apt: Jesus arrives as the conquering emperor to protect his people, and damn the rest. The book of Revelation makes this case of colonial mimicry most clear, but this eschatological concern is not anti-Roman on a practical level.

On the other hand, Jesus is by no means a Zealot in the sense Josephus describes them in that he is not advocating for an armed rebellion against Rome. Then again, not many people were in the late 20s and early 30s of the Common Era, as far as we know. The non-violent approach to Rome is standard practice: peaceful protest tends to be more effective when the protesters are facing an organized Roman army, an empire concerned that the taxes get paid, and an administration interested in keeping the peace.

John the Baptist was also a popular leader arrested by the local authority (Herod Antipas, in Galilee) and executed. Herod's concern was that John might lead the people into rebellion (i.e., revolution), and so he engaged in a pre-emptive strike (Josephus, *Antiquities* 18.118). But John's role was non-violent protest.

When Pilate 'sent by night those images of Caesar that are called Ensigns, into Jerusalem' (Josephus, *War* 2.169), the 'Jews' petitioned the governor in Caesarea to remove them. When Pilate refused, 'they fell down prostrate upon the ground, and continued immovable in that posture for five days and as many nights' (*War* 2.171). This may be history's first sit-down strike. When Pilate then threatens to send out his troops to massacre the strikers, 'Hereupon the Jews, as it were at one signal, fell down in vast numbers together, and exposed their necks bare, and cried out that they were sooner ready to be slain, than that their law should be transgressed' (*War* 2.174). Pilate concedes.

In the issue of the ensigns, we know what the people are protesting. It becomes more difficult to discern what exactly regarding Rome Jesus protested. Even the epithet given to one of his disciples – Simon who was called the zealot (*Simōna ton kaloumenon zēlōtēn*; Luke 6.15; Acts 1.13)—may not refer to his political affiliation or to his zeal for his tradition but to his zeal for the group he had joined. Everywhere else in the New Testament where that term is found, it concerns piety, not politics (Acts 21.20; 22.3; 1 Corinthians 14.12; Galatians 1.13; Titus 2.14; 1 Peter 3.13). Finally, Mark 3.18 and, following Mark, Matthew 10.4 refer to this same Simon as the '*Cananean*,' which means 'jealous' or 'zealous', but not, again, necessarily with political implications. Jesus the 'Zealot' is imaginative; it is also anachronistic, at best.

Finally, if Jesus did stand against Rome *qua* empire, it becomes difficult to determine why all of his followers, from whom we have records, did not follow suit. The only one who seems to have gotten this anti-Roman message is John, the author of Revelation. If John is writing *ca.* 69–70, which seems to me likely, then he has adapted his understanding of Jesus to a Diaspora setting, a case of Jesus-assemblies routinizing to the status quo (e.g., eating meat offered to idols, Revelation 2.20), and concluded that Rome is in fact the eschatological enemy. But that's John, not Jesus.

Revolution against Jewish particularism?

Alternatively, there is Jesus the revolutionary who overturns not the Roman but the Pharisaic status quo. The Gospels tell us that Pharisees follow the 'traditions of the elders' (cf. Matthew 15.2; Mark 7.3, 5) whereas Jesus speaks on his own authority and so brings something new, literally, to the table in rejecting handwashing. Here, the reverse is likely the case. The Pharisees are the ones who bring about a revolution in halakhic understanding by broadening the role of priest outside of one's lineage (priesthood in Jewish tradition is carried on the paternal line) and extending the model to the people as a whole. It is the Pharisees who, as Josephus puts it, 'delivered to the people a great many observances by succession from their fathers, which are not written in the law of Moses' (*Antiquities* 13.297), with many of these practices designed to promote the religious lives of Jews outside the priestly/Temple system. These practices then served to aid the Jewish people in preserving their ethnic identity following the destruction of the Temple in 70 C.E.

One variant of the Jesus-the-anti-Pharisaic revolutionary is the claim that Jesus does away with all of those ethnic markers – dietary restrictions, circumcision, Sabbath practices – in favour of a universalistic ethic. That argument doesn't work either, for at least four reasons. First, the claim that a universalistic perspective is a revolutionary advance on (tribal) particularism is a matter of ideology, not of fact. I frequently find the calls to universalism over-and-against particularity to be made by those in the majority; in such cases, the majority has nothing to lose, other than the benefits of diversity. The universalism that was proclaimed in the name of Jesus in which 'there is no longer

Jew or Greek, there is no longer slave or free, there is no longer male and female; for all of you are one in Christ Jesus' (Galatians 3.28) becomes simply a different form of particularism: the followers of Jesus and everyone else.

Second, Jesus does not do away with dietary regulations, Sabbath observance or anything else that served as markers of what we would call multiculturalism. Nor does Paul, since his teaching concerns Gentiles interested in proselyte conversion. Jesus is a halakhically observant Jew, who adheres to the dietary regulations, wears tzitzit, goes to synagogues, accepts the title son of David and calls the Temple his Father's house (if he so rejected it, it becomes impossible to understand why his followers continued to worship there and why Paul refers to Temple service [Romans 9.4, *latreia*] as a blessing to the Jews).

Third, nor again does Jesus invent universalism. Whether his statements in Matthew 10.5b–6 and 15.24 about being sent 'only to the lost sheep of the house of Israel' are authentic or are pieces of Matthean redaction (and I strongly suspect the latter), he does not engage in a Gentile mission. His focus may be 'sinners and tax collectors', but those sinners and tax collectors are all Jews. There are no Gentiles among the Twelve, and while some may have followed him in order to benefit from a healing or an exorcism, his focus is not on them.

If Jesus saw himself as a messiah (as he likely did), a Gentile mission would not likely have occurred to him. While Jews had a variety of beliefs about the messianic age, one dominant one was that it would result in the turning of Gentiles from their native religious practices (what the biblical texts refer to as 'idolatry') and their turning toward the God of Israel. It was not the job of the Messiah to bring about the conversion of the Gentiles: that conversion would be done by divine fiat, as would the resurrection of the dead and the ingathering of the exiles.

Two texts should suffice as evidence. Isaiah 2.2 proclaims, 'In days to come the mountain of the Lord's house shall be established as the highest of the mountains, and shall be raised above the hills; all the nations shall stream to it' (cf. 9.1; 11.10, 12; 12.4; 25.7; 34.1; 42.1; 43.9; 49.6; 55.5; 60.3, 11; 61.11; 66.18, 20); Zechariah 8.23 predicts, 'Thus says the LORD of hosts: In those days ten men from nations of every language shall take hold of a Jew, grasping his garment and saying, "Let us go with you, for we have heard that God is with you."' No need for a messiah here, or even for evangelists: the nations (i.e., Gentiles) spontaneously shift the focus of their worship.

The messianic age proclaimed by Jesus' followers should have brought in the Gentiles. But because the other signs of the messianic age – a general resurrection of the dead; the return of Jews in the Diaspora, including the 'ten lost tribes', to the land of Israel, a final judgement, peace on earth, etc. – did not occur, Jesus' followers then took the next logical step: in the interval, they began to proclaim his resurrection and so the start of the messianic age among the Gentiles.

Ironically, while the advocates of the anti-Pharisaic revolutionary Jesus typically rejoice in multiculturalism, the one particularism they do not like is Jewish particularism.

Ethical revolution?

In terms of ethics, Jesus has several helpful things to say, but I am not convinced they are revolutionary. If they are, then it's distressing that neither he nor his followers generally acted upon them. Here are four examples of the argument that his ethical programme was 'revolutionary' and their counters.

First is the claim that the so-called 'antitheses' in the Sermon on the Mount – the 'you have heard it said. . . but I say to you' offer a revolutionary ethic. The initial problem is that the term 'antithesis' is incorrect, as we see with Matthew 5.21–22, the first example: 'You have heard that it was said to those of ancient times, "You shall not murder"; and "whoever murders shall be liable to judgment". But I say to you that if you are angry with a brother, you will be liable to judgment; and if you insult a brother, you will be liable to the council; and if you say, "You fool," you will be liable to the Gehenna of fire.' The statement is not antithetical. An antithetical statement would be 'you have heard it said, "Do not murder," but I say to you, "kill as many people as you like."' Next, Jesus is doing the same thing that rabbinic Judaism does in 'building a fence about the law' (cf. Pirke Avot 1.1): to avoid breaking one law, build a fence around it to protect it. We even see how this process works out in the rabbis' legislation that makes capital punishment almost impossible to implement.

Even the famous 'eye for an eye' vs. 'turn the other cheek' (Matthew 5.38–39) is not an antithesis. An antithesis would be to give the offender the second eye. Rather, here Jesus changes the subject. There is a world of difference between losing a limb and being given a backhanded slap. Thus, Jesus never addresses what the appropriate response to murder or to the loss of a limb would be. Compounding the misunderstanding of the talion: Jews did not practice it as far as we know. The law serves both to prevent the escalation of violence (cf. Genesis 4.24) and to equalize the legal system across social classes (contrast the code of Hammurabi).

Second is the claim that the Golden Rule – 'In everything do to others as you would have them do to you; for this is the law and the prophets' (Matthew 7.12, cf. Luke 6.31) – epitomizes the best of an ethical system. It doesn't, as philosophers since Kant have noted. It presumes that our desires are shared by everyone else; it has given licence to missionaries to take indigenous children away from their parents, forbid them to speak in their own languages and worship in their own tradition, and otherwise become 'good Christians', for that is what the missionaries wanted for themselves. The Golden Rule is a good start, but as many have observed, it is neither unique nor unproblematic. The connection to the Torah and the Prophetic texts, and their interpretation, is the necessary next step, although in citations of the Golden Rule, the second part of the verse goes missing.

The so-called Silver Rule takes the negative formulation. The book of Tobit, which antedates Jesus, depicts the titular character, an ancient Jewish Polonius, advising his son with, 'Do not keep over until the next day the wages of those who work for you, but pay them at once. If you serve God you will receive payment. Watch yourself, my son, in everything you do, and discipline yourself in all your conduct. And what you hate, do not do to anyone. Do not drink wine to excess or let drunkenness go with you on your way' (Tobit 4.14–15). The Silver Rule is conventional wisdom.

An alternative version of the Silver Rule is ascribed to the teacher Hillel, a slightly older contemporary of Jesus, who, when asked by a Gentile to summarize the entire Torah 'while standing on one foot', replied, 'That which is hateful to you do not do to another; that is the entire Torah, and the rest is its interpretation. Go study' (b. Shabbat 31a). The Silver Rule too is insufficient without the rest of Tobit's wisdom sayings or Hillel's tradition.

Third is the view that Jesus expands the love command in Leviticus from neighbour to anyone in need and so dismisses ethnic concerns. This too is not quite right. Jesus quotes, as part of his 'great commandment', Leviticus 19.18, 'You shall love your neighbour as yourself' (Matthew 22.39; Mark 12.31). In Romans 13.9 and Galatians 5.14, Paul repeats this verse, which suggests it has its origins with Jesus. James 2.8 does the same.

My students repeatedly argue that Jews would have seen the Levitical mandate as related only to fellow Jews, but Jesus extends it to others. In making this claim, they yank Leviticus 19.18 out of context, even as they dismiss their own political concerns and ecclesial practices. 'Neighbour' in Leviticus 19.18 does mean fellow Jew. However, Leviticus does not limit this love only to Jews. Leviticus 19.34 also mandates, 'The alien who resides with you shall be to you as the citizen among you; you shall love the alien as yourself, for you were aliens in the land of Egypt.' Those Egyptians were the very people who enslaved the Israelites and then drowned their male babies; loving such aliens would take some effort.

In Luke's Gospel, the love command shows up not on the lips of Jesus, but in a lawyer's response to him (Luke 10.27b). This is the run-up to the parable of the Good Samaritan, when the lawyer then asks Jesus, 'Who is my neighbour?' (Luke 10.29). Samaritans were the test case for insider vs. outsider: were they to be seen as 'Jews' or as 'not-Jews'? Josephus gives one example of a long-standing debate: 'for such is the disposition of the Samaritans, as we have already elsewhere declared, that when the Jews are in adversity they deny that they are of kin to them, and then they confess the truth; but when they perceive that some good fortune hath befallen them, they immediately pretend to have communion with them, saying, that they belong to them, and derive their genealogy from the posterity of Joseph, Ephraim, and Manasseh' (*Antiquities* 11.341).

By asking 'who is my neighbour', the lawyer poses a very good question. Neighbours share the same rights and responsibilities; strangers do not. Therefore, we need to determine who our neighbour is (e.g., a citizen of our country, with the right to vote; a member of a particular church, with the right to participate in the Eucharist; a student enrolled in our classes, with the right to earn course credit) and who is the stranger. Jesus does not broaden the category of neighbour. Rather, as with the talion, he changes the subject. At the end of the parable, the question goes from who 'is' a neighbour to who 'acted' as a neighbour.

One could make the case that Jesus is revolutionary in his mandate to love the enemy (Matthew 5.44). The commandment is another form of fence building: Jesus builds a fence around loving neighbours and strangers by extending to loving the enemy. The problem here is that he, along with many of his followers over the centuries, has a peculiar way of showing it. To those who do not accept his message, or his messianic identity (the two tend to merge), including entire cities, he issues woe oracles (Matthew 11.21; Luke 10.13); the invectives against the Pharisees in Matthew 23 sound less loving and more condemnatory (my students tell me this is 'tough love'; to me, calling people a 'brood of vipers' is not indicative of a loving approach).

Nor is the statement without precedent. Proverbs 24.17 enjoins: 'Do not rejoice when your enemies fall, and do not let your heart be glad when they stumble', and Proverbs 25.21–22 mandates, 'If your enemies are hungry, give them bread to eat; and if they are thirsty, give them water to drink'. Granted, the rationale is not to turn enemies into friends but to frustrate them, 'for you will heap coals of fire on their heads, and the Lord will reward you'. In Romans 12.20, Paul quotes this verse. On loving enemies, Jeremiah also comes close. He instructs the community in Babylon, 'Seek the welfare of the city where I have sent you into exile, and pray to the Lord on its behalf, for in its welfare you will find your welfare' (Jeremiah 29.7). Love needs to be manifest, and Proverbs and Jeremiah gives forms of its manifestation: food, drink and prayer.

Finally, Jesus' rationale for his teaching, 'Love your enemies and pray for those who persecute you' (Matthew 5.44) is that 'so that you may be children of your Father in heaven' who is concerned about the righteous and the unrighteous alike (5.45).

The idea of modelling behaviour after that of the perfect God appears also in the rabbinic tradition, 'Just as He is compassionate and merciful, so too should you be compassionate and merciful' (b. Shabbat 133b).

Fourth is the claim that Jesus' ethic, indeed his entire programme, is designed to speak for the marginal, the outcast and the despised. The problem here is the vagueness of the terms. This is the approach that gets us Jesus the social revolutionary, a combination of Paulo Freire and Karl Marx, Martin Luther (on one of his better days), Paolo Pasolini's Jesus (with his hints of Ernesto "Che" Guevara) and a few others (usually men). The terms 'marginal' and 'outcast', often accompanied by 'poor' and 'destitute', become associated with those to whom Jesus ministers, and his approach is seen as 'radical'. In turn, this concern for the outcast and the marginal becomes the reason why Jesus is killed, just like Mahatma Gandhi, Martin Luther King Jr., Harvey Milk, Oscar Romero, Dorothy Stang and countless others.

The problem is that the texts do not support the claim. To speak about the 'marginal' and the 'outcast' we first need to determine who fits into the categories, and that means asking 'marginal to what?' and 'cast out by whom?' Jesus' inner circle are not the marginal, defined economically: Peter, Andrew, James and John are in the fishing business, with James and John the sons of a man who also has hired hands in his employ. Jesus is frequently seen dining not with the poor and marginal but with the rich and well connected. People follow him less because he proclaims good news to the poor (what that 'good news' is remains usually undefined), but because he is a healer and an exorcist, and free medical care is appreciated across the class system. His comments about the evils of hoarding money and ignoring the poor are nothing new, as a journey from Deuteronomy through all the prophetic literature quickly shows.

Jesus does engage in what looks like voluntary poverty, and to one potential disciple he does advise, 'Sell all that you own and distribute the money to the poor, and you will have treasure in heaven; then come, follow me' (Luke 18.22 cf. Matthew 19.21; Mark 10.21). The commandment is a one-off, and the rich man cannot accept it. Selling all one has is fine on the individual level (providing the seller does not have a family to support); on the communal level, it sets up a system that eventually collapses, as we see with the communitarian gathering in Acts 1—6.

Nor does his association with people in states of ritual impurity make him revolutionary, despite the enormous popularity of this view. When Jesus touches a man suffering from leprosy and heals him, he is not being either revolutionary or halakhically aberrant; he is being kind. He then sends the man to the Temple to make the requisite sacrifice (a point that also indicates that the fellow, although suffering from leprosy, has the funds to get to the Temple and make the offering; Matthew 8.4; Mark 1.44; Luke 5.14). When a woman suffering from haemorrhages touches him and feels in her body that her bleeding has stopped, he does not do away with purity laws. Rather, as with the man suffering from leprosy, he restores the woman to ritual purity. When he touches a corpse, he becomes ritually impure, but so what? Impurity does not disrupt daily life. Despite the popularity of the claim that Jesus treats impurity lightly or dismisses it entirely (a claim that fits the distaste for Jewish particularity), it is supported by no biblical text.

Jesus does have women serving in a patronage capacity in his entourage (see Luke 8.1-3), and all the Gospels report the presence of the women at the cross and the tomb. But women in Second Temple Judaism are not marginal or outcast: some were patrons of Pharisees; they have access to their own funds and they independently own houses; they have freedom of travel; they appear in synagogues and in the Temple. Jesus is not revolutionary in having women following him, or in healing their bodies. Had he put a woman among the Twelve, a better case for a revolutionary act could be made. Indeed, had he set up a system where ideas were shared and individuals got credit for their contribution to the whole, he would have been revolutionary. Instead, he substitutes one form of leadership (the tetrarch, the governor, the father) for another: his own.

Perhaps had Jesus welcomed slaves as equals into his group, he might be seen as revolutionary (Jesus as Spartacus, or even Kirk Douglas). Instead, he uses the language of slaves in his parables and so accepts the system rather than combats it. In the biblical tradition, free people typically accept the designation 'slave' of God, as we see, e.g., in Mary's famous comment, 'Behold the handmaid of the Lord; be it unto me according to thy word' (KJV); the Greek translated 'handmaid' is *doulē*, 'slave'. To tell a rich or privileged person, 'be a slave' or at least minister to others is appropriate. To tell a slave, who has no choice in the matter, 'Be a slave' is not a note of freedom.

Jesus does associate with 'tax collectors and sinners', and with this group we can use terms like 'marginal', but only in a very select way. When I think of people 'on the margins' today, I think of those without shelter, who have food insecurity, who do not know if they can make the rent, who are living on the streets or in shelters. Those readings are a far cry from the 'sinners and tax collectors'. Their marginalization exists only in that they remove themselves from communal welfare in order to make money. Tax collectors work for the Romans; 'sinners' do not refer to people who eat a pork chop or knit an afghan on the Sabbath. Sinners would be the ancient equivalents of drug dealers, arms traders, and wealthy men caught in the #MeToo movement. They are not the poor and exploited; they are the rich and uncaring. It is courageous of Jesus to try to bring this group to repentance, but it is not revolutionary.

Related to the marginal and outcast model is the claim that the Temple incident functioned to protest the exploitation of the laity, here with a focus on the moneychangers (which many think are moneylenders, and thus importing a host of other anti-Jewish stereotypes into the text). However, the Temple incident is not about economics. Mark gives the initial version, which indicates not an economic focus but a concern to stop all Temple activity:

> . . . he entered the temple and began to drive out those who were selling and those who were buying in the temple, and he overturned the tables of the money changers and the seats of those who sold doves; and he would not allow anyone to carry anything through the temple. He was teaching and saying, Is it not written, 'My house shall be called a house of prayer for all the nations'? But you have made it a den of robbers. (Mark 11.15b–17).

If no one could carry anything, then no one could make an offering (as with the widow's two coins, and those who were able to give more, cf. Mark 12.41–44).

'Den of robbers' does not mean a place where the poor are exploited. The term is a quote from Jeremiah, who speaks about people who participate in the rituals but who do not demonstrate fidelity in their daily practices. Jeremiah condemns those whose Temple appearance marks their hypocrisy: 'Here you are, trusting in deceptive words to no avail. Will you steal, murder, commit adultery, swear falsely, make offerings to Baal, and go after other gods that you have not known, and then come and stand before me in this house, which is called by my name, and say, "We are safe!"—only to go on doing all these abominations? Has this house, which is called by my name, become a den of robbers in your sight? You know, I too am watching, says the LORD' (Jeremiah 7.8–11). The subject is hypocrisy, not economics.

In John's version of this scene, retrojected from the beginning of the Passion Narrative to early in the mission, after Jesus changes water into wine at Cana, the quote changes. John states, 'Making a whip of cords, he drove all of them out of the temple, both the sheep and the cattle. He also poured out the coins of the money changers and overturned their tables. He told those who were selling the doves, "Take these things out of here! Stop making my Father's house a marketplace!"' (John 2.15–16). The subject is eschatology, not economics. The quotation alludes to Zechariah 14.21: 'and every cooking pot in Jerusalem and Judah shall be sacred to the LORD of hosts, so that all who sacrifice may come and use them to boil the flesh of the sacrifice. And there shall no longer be traders in the house of the LORD of hosts on that day.' In John's Christology, there is no longer any need for the sacrificial system or the Temple, because Jesus' body replaces the practice and the institution. John makes his point palpable two chapters later, when Jesus tells the Samaritan woman, 'Woman, believe me, the hour is coming when you will worship the Father neither on this mountain nor in Jerusalem. . . .. But the hour is coming, and is now here, when the true worshipers will worship the Father in spirit and truth, for the Father seeks such as these to worship him' (John 4.21, 23).

Some might take these words from John, combine them with Mark's apocalyptic perspective (see esp. Mark 13), and conclude that Jesus was revolutionary in his eschatological approach. Anyone who teaches that the end of the world is coming, who advises his followers to pray, 'Your kingdom come' and so rejects the kingdom in which they are presently living, who pulls children away from parents, husbands away from wives, who sets up a fictive kinship group in which one's mother and brothers and sisters are related by loyalty to him rather than to their natal families, and who proclaims himself divinely commissioned is setting up an alternative way of living. There is nothing original here, and it is not clear to me that it is something I'd want to promulgate. The message did not much take hold among the majority of Jews in Judea or Galilee; it did have a greater appeal to the Gentiles, in that it offered them eternal life without cost (something Jews already had as part of their soteriological system, in large measure thanks to the Pharisees). More, its followers promised support to those who lacked it.

Those who experienced Jesus as raised from the dead found their worlds changed. No longer was Simon the fisherman in Galilee; he was now Peter, running a movement in Jerusalem. Paul goes from being an opponent of the movement to being its greatest apostle. Meanwhile, the message morphs from a focus on praxis to a focus on doctrine; the eschatological urgency gives way, in general, to routinization. The Gentile followers, originally a problem for their turning from the worship of idols (as Jews would describe pagan practice) to the worship of the God of Israel, accommodated to the Roman system by going through the motions of expected behaviour (see 1 Peter 2.11–17).

We do not need Jesus to tell us to feed the hungry, provide medical care, treat others with the same respect as we would like to be treated, or even see everyone – neighbour, stranger, enemy – as in the image of the divine. The message of care is already part of Deuteronomy.

Story as revolution

To start a revolution, it helps to have a good story. Jesus has multiple good stories. To define the revolution, it helps to determine the target. Jesus was not unaware of politics and economics, of non-violent revolution and a concern for forgiving debts. But he was also interested in preparing his followers to live as if they already had one foot in the kingdom of heaven. He does so in various ways: instruction, modelling action, sharing his visions. He does so as well by telling stories. The parables prompt us to see the world otherwise; they help us question our presuppositions; they activate not only imagination but response. The more I look at the parables, the better I am able to ask the right questions and to recognize the ambiguities of life. Thus I can attest that the parables – more accurately, interpreting the parables – has turned my world upside down (cf. Acts 17.6) by bringing to the surface what I know to be true and right, but what I try to ignore or forget.

The reception history of the parables repeats the act of domestication. The parables become children's stories, and the parents and teachers do not find the children capable of deep moral reasoning. Thus the parables become robbed of their provocation: the Prodigal Son means that God loves people who sin or make mistakes; the Good Samaritan means we help people who are not part of our group, or 'those people' (the 'other') are nice too.

For the church fathers, the parables often become allegories, with the writer holding the answer key. They, like the entire 'Old Testament', are seen primarily as making Christological points. Ethics yields to doxa. The parables then become morality tales, a move already started by the Evangelists. For Luke, the parable of the widow and the judge is about praying always and not losing heart (Luke 18.1) and not about a very complex story of a widow who asks for vengeance and a judge who grants her desire not because it is just but because she threatens him with an uppercut. The parables of the lost sheep and the lost coin are, for Luke, about repenting and forgiving (Luke 15.4–10), despite the facts that the sheep-owner (never called a shepherd) and the woman lost, respectively, their sheep and coin, that sheep and coins do not repent, and that the owner and the woman do not forgive their lost objects.

Praying always is fine advice (it couldn't hurt), and reading the parables of lost sheep and coin, along with the third parable in the triptych of Luke 15, the 'prodigal son', as about repenting and forgiving is fine too. I've been teaching for over two decades in a maximum-security prison in Nashville, and for a number of my insider students who identify with the prodigal, they find solace in knowing that God (the father) will receive them. I would not take that reading away from them, and I think that Jesus would concur. I do not think, however, that the idea of a forgiving God is either new (the Golden Calf was not one of Israel's better moments, but the covenant continues; of course Jews believe in a God who forgives) or that, in fact, the father 'forgave' the prodigal, for there was nothing technically to 'forgive'. Despite his interior monologue about claiming to have sinned, he did nothing more than engage in 'dissolute living': to be stupid is not the same thing as to be sinful.

In the parable of the man who had two sons (Luke 15.11–32), traditionally the 'parable of the Prodigal Son', the opening line sends me back to similar stories of men with two sons in the antecedent texts: Adam the father of Cain and Abel, Abraham the father of Ishmael and Isaac, Isaac the father of Esau and Jacob, and so on (there are others). In all cases, the narrative favours the younger son, and in all cases, the older brother was treated unfairly, whether by God or by his parents. In all cases, the fathers fail, either because they are absent or because they show favouritism. In Jesus' parable, the father fails the older brother: he had enough time to arrange music and dancing, and invite the neighbours to celebrate the prodigal's return, but he forgot to invite the older brother. Finally, in this story, the father realizes his mistake and goes out to plead with his elder. And so I return to reclaim Cain and Ishmael and Esau, who are also part of the family.

In its narrative context in Luke 15, the parable does more. When we strip out the Lucan insistence on repenting and forgiving (again, nothing wrong with either), we get a better message, and one typically missed by Christian interpreters. In the first parable, the man has 100 sheep and loses one. The only way to determine a missing sheep is to count them. In the second parable, the woman has ten coins and loses one. Again, the only way to know that one coin out of ten is lost is to count. In the third parable, we go from 100 to ten to two: there was a man who had two sons. His problem: he forgot to count the older brother. And so we realize the importance of making everyone feel counted, especially those who are overlooked: the dutiful child who does everything right while the sibling (disabled, on drugs, a brilliant athlete, a musical genius) absorbs all of the father's attention; the quiet student who neither shines nor demands remedial help. More, we realize that people are not sheep or coins: they are human beings who have emotional responses that must be addressed. Once these lessons come to our consciousness, we become better parents, better teachers, better human beings.

When we go back to the widow and the judge, we find how easy it is to slip from the desire for justice to the desire for vengeance, a desire already demonstrated by the majority of the translations of Luke 18.3: 'In that city there was a widow who kept coming to him and saying, "Grant me justice against my opponent"' (NRSV). The Greek literally has her ask, 'avenge me against my adversary' (*ekdikēson me apo tou antidikou mou*). The opening term *ekdikēson* is the same word that appears in the famous statement, 'Vengeance is mine, says the Lord' (Romans 12.19, quoting Deuteronomy 32.35; see also 2 Corinthians 10.6; Revelation 6.10; 19.2 – nothing about 'justice' here; the same connotation holds for uses in the Septuagint).

As for the widow and her opponent, she is doing the opposite of what the Sermon on the Mount demands: 'Come to terms quickly with your accuser while you are on the way to court with him, or your accuser may hand you over to the judge, and the judge to the guard, and you will be thrown into prison' (Matthew 5.25; Luke 12.58). The fourth and last time the term appears in the New Testament is 1 Peter 5.8, 'Discipline yourselves, keep alert. Like a roaring lion your adversary (*antidikos*), the devil prowls around, looking for someone to devour' (NRSV). No reconciliation with Satan here either.

The parable, detached from its Lucan frame, does what a good parable, a revolutionary story, should do. It upsets our stereotypes and our standards. Can we side with the widow, stereotyped along with the poor, the orphan, and the stranger (e.g., Deuteronomy 10.18; 24.19–21; 27.19), as vulnerable and in need of protection, or do we see her as rich, demanding, and bent on vengeance (cf. Judith)? Do we even notice the opponent, or do we pre-determine that his case is unjust? Does the judge, who grants the widow her request not for reasons of justice but for self-preservation, do the right thing for the wrong reason, or the wrong thing for the right reason? What is the difference between justice and vengeance (a question several of my insider students, serving long or life sentences, have asked)? To ask such questions is to refuse the stereotype, the status quo, and the uninformed opinion.

For a third example of thinking otherwise, the parable of the Pearl of Great Price (Matthew 13.45–46) raises, in Stoic fashion, the question of importance: 'the kingdom of heaven is like a merchant in search of fine pearls; on finding one pearl of great value, he went and sold all that he had and bought it.' The pearl need not have a single allegorical interpretation (the Cross, eternal life, the church, discipleship), and most of the allegorical interpretations would not have made sense to a first-century Jewish audience. The parable is ridiculous on the surface: the merchant (*emporos*), hardly the type of job that would be associated with godly rule, cf. Revelation 18.3, 11, 15, 23 as well as Sirach 26.29; 37.11) sells everything he has to buy a pearl. At this point, he is no longer a merchant: he is a fellow with a pearl, and nothing else. And yet he has what he wants. He is no longer acquisitive; he has sold (no mention of 'sacrifice') everything else, and he is happy. He knows for him what matters, regardless of how ridiculous his choice is to anyone else. To consider this merchant is to consider what we need vs. what we want; what we choose rather than what has been chosen for us.

Finally, the parable of the Dishonest Steward (Luke 16.1–8a), stripped again of its Lucan contextualization, raises the question of morality. In this parable, no one behaves morally. The rich man (parables about rich men usually end badly for the rich man) believes the gossip and does not give the steward the chance of explaining his situation; he also fails to collect the books from the steward. The steward, who is too proud to beg (at that comment, I lose sympathy for him), cheats his master out of some of the debts; the debtors would have known that something illegal was afoot in the steward's initial question of how much they owed (he had the books; he would know the amount) and then his insistence that they quickly write down lower numbers. In the end, the master commends the steward. Why? Because although no one behaved well, everyone benefited. The steward keeps his job; the master gets a reputation for generosity; the debtors owe less. We are thus forced to think about means and ends, whether making the rich a bit less rich is a good thing, and at what point on the economic scale is cheating someone out of a debt, appropriate: in all cases, since we are to 'forgive debts' (Matthew 6.12b) and 'give to anyone who begs' (Luke 6.30)?

The other parables pose the same type of important questions, if we would only listen to them without the allegorical or

Christological frosting with which they today come packaged. Short stories that make us think, that make us question ethics and economics, need and desire, justice and vengeance, our ancestral texts and our present relations, can revolutionize the way we live. If we only had ears to hear.

Jesus Christ, game changer

NICK SPENCER

I grew up in a non-Christian household. My parents weren't anti-Christian, simply not interested – put off faith for life by a convent education and by public school hypocrisies. I left for university to study English literature and history. My parents steeled themselves, as parents of adolescent graduates do, for a messy, sophomoric entanglement with drink, drugs or women. Three years later, I came back an Anglican. They didn't know what to do.

In truth, the journey had started several years earlier, not that I really realized it at the time. Poetry was to blame. At 14, I had been blessed with a brilliant, inspirational English teacher, who rescued the subject from the pointless tedium of 'comprehensions' and introduced me to writers who demanded much but offered more. (The whole process was aided and abetted by the opportunity to do a 100 per cent coursework GSCE, which gave us bewildering freedom and bounty; I sigh when I think of the exam-obsessed, rote-quote-learning nightmare that my children have had to endure by comparison.)

My teacher introduced me to a wide range of authors and texts, but, time and again, it was the poets and poems that wrestled with the pain of faith and doubt that captivated me. I encountered John Donne's theatrically-tortured holy sonnets, his haranguing *A Hymn to God the Father* and his self-conscious *Good Friday 1613. Riding Westwards.* I read George Herbert's remarkably modern *Prayer (1)* and his divine ventriloquism in *Love (3).* I was transported by Matthew Arnold's

Dover Beach and his *Stanzas from the Grand Chartreuse*. I chewed on Arthur Hugh Clough's grief-stricken *Easter Day. Naples, 1849* ('Christ is not risen, no,/ He lies and moulders low;'), Gerard Manley Hopkins' dark sonnets ('No worst, there is none') and, with great difficulty, his *Wreck of the Deutschland*. I was moved by Wordsworth's *Tintern Abbey*, Seamus Heaney's *In Illo Tempore,* Larkin's more phlegmatic *Church Going*, Derek Walcott's *Return to D'Ennery; Rain*, and Geoffrey Hill's incomprehensibly beautiful *Lachrimae*. These were utterly different minds and moods. Larkin hasn't much in common with Donne, and Clough's *Easter Day* is a world away from Herbert's *Love*. But they all converged on the idea that this stuff mattered. Whatever else you might think of belief in the Christian God, it was something that demanded attention.

Above and beyond all these, however, the poet whose work I found most tantalizing was T. S. Eliot. This will not surprise. Eliot is the literary Christian's poet of choice, his *Ash Wednesday* and his *Four Quartets* achieving a quasi-scriptural status for many a believer, especially the Anglican ones. But it was neither of those discursively Christian sequences that captured me, but his altogether more troubled, fragmentary and difficult modernist classic *The Waste Land*.

Like many (every?) a reader, I had little idea what the poem actual meant when I first read it, but like so many other poems of faith and doubt I had read, I sensed it grappling with something profoundly important. Its savage urban forays and troubled encounters arrested me, as did what the thunder gnomically said, in the poem's final section, as the speaker's spiritual journey stumbles to an unsatisfying conclusion:

What have we given?
My friend, blood shaking my heart

The awful daring of a moment's surrender
Which an age of prudence can never retract
By this, and only this, we have existed.

The poem searches for redemption, seeing signs and hearing echoes of it before ultimately collapsing into incoherence, leaving the reader only with fragments to shore up or scatter as they please. One of these fragments was the awful daring of a moment's surrender, an idea that haunted me.

Revolutionary expectations in the first century

I begin on this atypically personal note because, ultimately, all encounters with or rejections of Jesus Christ are personal ones. Christianity is a personal invitation over and above (although not to the exclusion of) being a set of propositions about the existence of God, the meaning of life or the historicity of particular events.

As it happens, I also read a great deal of history at university, which did enable me, for the first time, to assess the historicity of the New Testament. Having naturally assumed that these documents were little more than untrustworthy pools of congealed Christian whispers, I was surprised by and impressed with their historical reliability. All of a sudden it became much harder to dismiss Christianity, which I had obviously done beforehand.

Whether trusted or dismissed, 'Christianity' hinged ultimately on what I thought of the person at its centre, and that person emerged as revolutionary, although not in the way I then understood the term. In 1999, the Churches Advertising Network (with which, for full disclosure, I became connected as an advisor many years later) ran a famous Easter campaign with a mocked up face of Jesus Christ/Che Guevara under which ran the line 'Meek. Mild. As if.' The campaign provoked much controversy, a few conservative and more Conservative believers frothing at the association. Regardless of what you think of its execution (you can still find the poster online and make up your own mind), the campaign drew on a well-worn idea of who was a revolutionary and what he (and the caricature was inevitably a he) did. Revolutionaries catalyse. They cause major, dramatic change, usually in the political arena. They do so through action. They are always provocative, frequently coercive, sometimes violent.

Che Guevara may be the most familiar revolutionary of modern generations, courtesy of a thousand student walls, but the idea of this kind of revolutionary is as old as the hills in which such figures are wont to hide. Such revolutionaries were familiar figures in first century Palestine. Indeed, it is hardly an exaggeration to say that revolution hung in the air everyone breathed, like dense fog.

Ever since the Maccabean revolt in the second century BC, the ingredients of revolution had been brewing away. First, and obviously, there was a deep-running and visceral hostility to foreign occupying powers, whether Greek, Roman or Jewish, which were deemed illegitimate. Second, and on the other side of that coin, there was fierce loyalty to God and his gift of the Torah, a loyalty that expressed itself in a holy one-upmanship in which different groups paraded their fidelity and policed others' waywardness. Third, there was a febrile expectation of God's intervention, a conviction that God not only had not abandoned his chosen people but that, Aslan-like, was on the move, ready to act on behalf of his patient, suffering people. Finally, there was a willingness to resort to violence, not simply because revolution was a habitually violent affair, but because the people knew that God would come as a conqueror. Everyone lived in the glorious shadow of the heroic martyrs of the Maccabean rebellion in the war against the Seleucid dynasty and the Hellenization of their culture. They knew what revolution demanded, and what it could cost. This was a potent mix.

For all that his intent was to excuse his people before the Romans, the Jewish historian Josephus brims over with tales of would-be revolutionaries and their failed revolutions. Some were small scale, acts of revolutionary vandalism more than large scale insurgencies. Josephus tells the story of how, as the widely disliked client king Herod the Great lay dying, two respected teachers of law, Judas ben Sepphoris and Matthias ben Margalus, egged on their young pupils to pull down the golden eagle that Herod had erected over the great gate of the temple. This was, they declared, 'a very proper time to defend the cause of God', and it would be 'a glorious thing to die for the laws of their country'. (*Wars* 1.648) This was hardly likely to bring Rome to its knees, but, focused on the Jerusalem Temple, it was a strategic strike at the inner reactor core of the religious edifice; flag burning outside the Oval Office for its time.

Other rebellions were more substantial but took place further afield. In the following book of his *Wars*, Josephus describes how 2,000 of Herod's veterans rebelled 'against. . .the king's party' in Idumea; how a Judas, son of 'arch-robber' Hezekias (who had also been executed for brigandage: it was obviously the family business) had broken into the royal armoury and led a revolt in Sepphoris, Galilee; and how, in Perea, Simon, a royal servant, had crowned himself before going about in a 'company of robbers' and burning down the royal palace at Jericho. (*Wars*, 2.55-57) How close any of these rebellions came to shaking the Romans is debateable though 'not very' seems the likely answer. But they were the revolutionary weather of the age.

Such weather was not made any better by the frequently brutal response by Roman governors and their troops. In the mere ten years of his time in Judea, we know that Pontius Pilate tried (and failed) to bring Roman standards into Jerusalem; used Temple funds to build an aqueduct (crushing any resistance in the process); sent in troops to kill some Galileans while they were offering sacrifices in the Temple; provoked popular anger by placing Roman votive shields in the Jerusalem palace; and savagely suppressed an (apparently non-revolutionary) prophetic movement in Samaria, for which he was finally sent back to Rome.[1] The Roman response to revolutionary sentiments was not to sit down and discuss legitimate grievances. It is small wonder that the crowds wanted revolution.

There is an important caveat to be made here. Just because there was so much violent revolutionary sentiment in the air at the time, that doesn't necessarily mean that all revolution was violent. The category of prophetic activity could overlap with violent revolution – after all, such revolutionaries were acting in God's name, by God's command and indeed on God's behalf – but it wasn't coterminous with it. John the Baptist was a menace, though not because of any propensity to murder or destroy. Words could threaten as much as swords, if only because the former all too often led to the latter.

These, then, were the revolutionary times in which Jesus lived. As Josephus remarked in his *Antiquities* (17.10.4) 'at this time there were ten thousand other disorders in Judea. . .because a great number put themselves into a warlike posture.' The *people* were expecting revolution of a kind. When Jesus rode into Jerusalem on what we now call Palm Sunday, he was greeted by crowds who were chanting royal verses about the return of their true ruler. The masses greeted him as their new king. They waved palm branches (at least according to John's account), recollecting the Feast of Tabernacles, which celebrated the dedication of the Temple and, more recently, Judas Maccabeus' cleansing of the Temple two centuries earlier. History was about to repeat itself.

The Temple authorities feared revolution of a kind. According to Luke, the chief priests shopped Jesus to Pilate on the basis that he was fomenting rebellion, refusing taxes (and therefore Caesar's authority) and claiming to be a king in his own right. In Luke's second volume, the books of Acts, he describes how the honoured Pharisee, Gamaliel, compared the nascent Jesus movement to the failed revolutions of Theudas and Judas the Galilean. (Acts 5.34-39)

The Roman authorities were prepared for revolution of a kind. According to the Gospels of Matthew, Mark and Luke, Jesus greets the Roman soldiers in Gethsemane with a phrase that underlines their perception of what was going on. 'Am I leading a rebellion,' he is recorded as saying, 'that you have come out with swords and clubs to capture me?' (Mark 14.48, Matthew 26.55, Luke 22.52) Roman soldiers came prepared for good reason, as they knew what revolution looked like.

And the Apostles themselves, or some of them for some of the time, were hoping for revolution of a kind. At least one of his disciples, Simon, was known as a Zealot, a revolutionary (some might say terrorist) sect of the time. Peter is prepared to take up arms to defend Jesus in Gethsemane. The disciples gleefully brandish multiple swords on the way to the Mount of Olives.

Jesus, then, was firmly placed and understood within the category of revolutionaries at the time. But he disappoints the crowds, frustrates the Temple authorities, hardly even registers with the Romans and stuns the Apostles when he reveals his true intent, saving some of his harshest words for Peter's denial – not of his master but of his master's intention to suffer and die in Jerusalem.

Jesus' revolution looks, on the surface of it, profoundly unrevolutionary. Contrary to the sabre-rattling, dagger-wielding, Roman-baiting, soldier-hating rhetoric and rage of his revolutionary contemporaries, Jesus advocates (and embraces) a rejection of all forms of compulsion, even when it comes at (an incalculable) personal cost. He seems broadly disinterested in occupying forces, although he is not above praising them for their faith (Matt. 8.12) or forgiving them for their ignorant cruelty (Luke 23.34). His attitude toward the occupying regime is one of assumed superiority rather than violent loathing. His fury, such as it is, is saved for his own people, or some of them, and their self-serving distortion of God's law. He deliberately avoids and evades the crowds who, now well fed, claim him as their prophet and try to 'make him king by force'. (John 6.15) His ethic is that of unqualified self-giving, which he requires of those who choose to follow him, demanding that they refuse wealth, status and power, and serve others instead. This is not the stuff of revolutionary rhetoric or combat. Indeed, given that he runs to the mountains to *avoid* the insurgent crowds in John 6, rather than drawing them there to plot an uprising, it is the very opposite of revolution.

None of this is to deny that Jesus acts with *authority*. Indeed, one of the most common reactions to him among the people was precisely that he did speak and act with authority that was absent or at least borrowed ('The law says. . .') by his priestly and teacherly contemporaries. Jesus forgives sins, apparently usurping the prerogative of priest and Temple, and even authorizes his disciples to do the same (Matt. 18.18, John 20.23) in a way that is presumably to be understood as a re-channelling of God's own authority. He conducts exorcisms, a common enough phenomenon at that time, but does so – uniquely – without using charms, amulets or spells, or without calling on some higher authority or power in order to do so. And he teaches in a way that eschews the familiar prophetic formula 'The words of the Lord says. . .' in favour of a resolute dependence on the first person singular. In the words of one New Testament scholar:

> In the age of Jesus there were plenty of parallels of people who laid claim to or whose office embodied the claim to divine authority: individuals who spoke in ecstasy in the person of the god who was thought to possess them; and kings whose very title expressed the claim to be manifestations of the deity. But there was nothing quite like this son of an artisan, who, in sober and wholly rational speech, claimed to speak for God as his representative at the end of the age; nothing quite like the unassuming arrogance of his egotism – 'But I say unto you. . .' (James Dunn, *The Partings of the Ways*, p. 239, SCM Press, 2011)

Jesus possessed authority but refused power. Small wonder that Peter (and the other apostles?) reacted the way he did when he first caught wind of Jesus' ultimate intentions. (Matt. 16.21-23) After all, you do not win a war by laying down all your weapons, you don't bring people to their knees by kneeling before them, you don't demonstrate glory as a convicted criminal – and you do not effect a revolution through the awful daring of a moment's surrender. Do you?

The depth of goodness

Yet, somehow this is what happened. There can be no serious doubt that Jesus Christ is the single most important figure in at least Western, arguably world, history, his minor movement creeping through and transforming the ancient world like some kind of metaphysical plague, which was pretty much what ancient and modern critics claim that it was. All on the foundation of a crucified messiah.

Why do we care? Why are we affected by the sight of the sacrificed Christ? Why do we not share Nietzsche's hearty contempt for Christianity's 'slave morality', his disdain for its founder's 'superficiality', his partiality for 'Olympus' over the 'crucified'? A preference for uncompromised strength and power is surely more "natural". It was hardly absent from the world in which Jesus lived – indeed, it was arguably the defining characteristic of that world – and is recognizable in cultures across the globe. Why are we sympathetic to the cross?

One argument, made recently by historians Tom Holland (in *Dominion*) and Alec Ryrie (in *Unbelievers*), is that this sympathy is simply a result of Christianity itself. We respect weakness, recognize innate rights, aspire to sacrifice, and so forth because we are children, or in some cases orphans, of Christianity. Our instinct is the legacy of 60 generations of the faith, dwelling in our moral bones.

I think that point is unarguable but still ultimately unsatisfactory. After all, it helps explain why some of the greater and lesser heretics of recent centuries – from Voltaire, Paine and Jefferson to Dawkins, P. Z. Myers and Philip Pullman – laud (or at least spare) Jesus in their otherwise indiscriminate criticism of Christianity. But it can hardly be a sufficient account as it fails to explain why the preaching of Christ crucified should have had any impact on a classical world as yet utterly untainted by any Christian legacy. It's one thing to say we are attracted to the revolutionary figure of Jesus because we still live in the shadow of his moral revolution, but quite another to say that first or second century Greeks and Romans were. There is, I think, something more profound going on here, something that connects with the deep moral order of creation.

At the end of his essay *The Abolition of Man*, C. S. Lewis appended a list of common ethical "laws", to be found across religious and non-religious traditions throughout history: the law of general benevolence, of special benevolence, of justice, veracity, mercy, magnanimity and so forth. It is a shock to some Christians who claim, erroneously, that there is something wholly unique about Christian morality. There may be something rather extreme in Jesus' ethic, particularly his forgiveness of enemies, but it turns out that humans inhabit broadly the same moral landscape and have often, though not always, prized the same course through it.

As it happens, that moral landscape goes far deeper than C. S. Lewis could have guessed. After decades, arguably centuries, in which the cognitive, affective and moral capacity of animals has been downplayed or altogether dismissed, ever more research is showing how plenty of animals (many only distantly related to one another) show signs of intelligence, emotions and ethics. Primates in particular (but not only primates: elephants, corvids and cephalopods also show clear signs of cognition) indicate that they are emotionally and ethically intelligent. Many show signs of what we would call moral awareness: of generosity, of reciprocity, and of first and second-order fairness – the former being a sense of whether I am being treated fairly, the latter of equity and justice in general – as well, of course, as shadow vices like jealously, vengeance and even guilt. Humans live and move and have our being in an ethical landscape every bit as real as the physical one. Good and evil pre-exist *Homo sapiens*. They go all the way down.

This is all very upsetting to those who confuse human dignity with human uniqueness, the idea that we are special because we are completely different from other creatures. The reality is that humans *are* different but more in degree rather than kind, more fully and knowingly immersed in the underlying moral order of creation, in which other species play in the shallows. Our difference lies in the fact that we are the creatures charged with knowing (and protecting and nurturing) the good that is embedded in creation, and which reflects its creator. In the words of the theologian Oliver O'Donovan, commenting on the second creation narrative in Genesis:

> It is man(kind) who gives the animals their names. Such a relationship to the rest of creation belongs to him in order that he may fulfil his own part in the universe by discerning and interpreting what he sees around him. Knowledge is the root of his authority over his fellow creatures. . . To know is to fill a quite specific place in the order or things, the place allotted to mankind. (O'Donovan, *Resurrection and Moral Order*, p. 81, IVP, 1994)

The problem is we're not very good at it – both knowing creation and ordering it – something that is popularly described by the problematically-blemished Christian word "sin". We have, in Francis Spufford's bracing formulation, a 'human propensity to fuck things up'.

Spufford's HPtFtu is a helpful translation of sin, but loses in precision what it gains in wit. We might, then, rephrase and reframe the problem in a way that helpfully clarifies it and illuminates the deep reasons why we are drawn to the awful daring of the cross.

The unveiling of animal morality over recent decades has been paralleled with the more theoretical understanding of the evolution of ethics, drawing heavily on "game theory". This was facilitated by the growth of computing power, which enables the iterative exploration of what happens when two moral agents engage with one another. How does each – or ideally both – get the best outcome possible? Innumerable strategies have been proposed, designed and tested, but it slowly emerged that an outrageously simple one, labelled "Tit-for-tat", in which each player paid back what they received in cooperation or betrayal, was the most successful for both parties. "Tit-for-tat" is a form of proportionate reward and equal retaliation. It is, in effect, the *lex talionis*, 'an eye for an eye', in modern terms. Doing to others as they do to you is the way things should be.

There was, however, a problem with "Tit-for-tat", as Matt Ridley, whose book *The Origins of Virtue* explores these issues, explained:

> there is a dark side to Tit-for-tat. . . if two Tit-for-tat players meet each other and get off on the right foot, they cooperate indefinitely. But if one of them accidentally or unthinkingly (let alone intentionally) defects, then a continuous series of mutual recriminations begins from which there is no escape. (Matt Ridley, *The Origins of Virtue*, p. 65, Viking, 1996)

More successful that Tit-for-tat, it slowly emerged, was a game strategy uncreatively called "Generous Tit-for-tat", in which one player forgives occasional lapses by the other, thereby preventing the whole game descending into an enduring blood feud. In effect, "Generous Tit-for-tat" instantiates forgiveness, turning the other cheek, as a way of rectifying a good relationship.

Instinctively, anyone who has ever been married, or been in a relationship, or had a good friend – so pretty much everyone really – gets this. You know damn well you were right in an argument, and they were wrong. The problem is, they think that too. And if you pursue your conviction of righteousness unapologetically and to the end, and they pursue theirs similarly, the marriage, relationship or friendship will grind itself into recrimination and revenge. The only way to restoration is to risk saying sorry – even though you're convinced you're not wrong, and even though the other person may not reciprocate, or may not accept your words with grace, or may not return with their own olive branch. Forgiving, apologizing, surrendering like this takes courage. You can even feel the blood shaking your heart as you do it. And yet we know in our rare moments of moral clarity that if we wish to sustain a relationship, rather than simply live alone in self-righteous solitude, it is by this, and only this, we will exist.

A revolution that changed the game

Talk of animal ethics and game theory may seem a country mile away from Jesus' revolutionary activities, but it is not. On the contrary, it helps illustrate precisely why he was so revolutionary. As we have seen, plenty of other revolutionaries jostled aggressively on the first-century Palestinian stage, but they wanted primarily to pay back the Romans' violence in kind, ideally with interest. Indeed, when Jesus replies to the question about paying taxes to Caesar – 'Render unto Caesar the things which are Caesar's; and unto God the things that are God's' in the Authorized Version – he may well have been referencing precisely that kind of tit-for-tat ethic found in the story of the Maccabean rebellion, in which Mattathias advises his sons to 'avenge the wrong done to your people (and) *pay back the Gentiles in full.*' (1 Macc. 2.66-68) Such revolutions wanted to change the actors, demoting the leads and putting some of the put-upon minor parts in charge. But it was the same play, the same game, the same rules.

Jesus' revolution, by contrast, was to change the script altogether. You have heard it said, but I say unto you, you are not longer to play Tit-for-tat. You are not even to play Generous Tit-for-tat, with its admirable but ultimately limited store of forgiveness. 'Lord, how many times shall I forgive my brother or sister who sins against me? Up to seven times?' 'I tell you, not seven times, but seventy-seven times.' (Matt. 18.22)

Moreover – and crucially – this isn't simply teaching. Whatever else you might say about Jesus, it's hard to criticize him for not practising what he preached. Indeed, his command to forgive makes no sense outside of his command to follow him. 'If anyone will come after me, let him deny himself, and take up his cross daily, and follow me.' (Luke 9.23) Jesus doesn't command forgiveness. His sacrifice *is* forgiveness. He simply asks us to join him.

Game theory may be more than just an illuminating metaphor in all this. Returning to that misunderstood and unpopular idea of "sin", we might say, borrowing the language of game theory, that human sin resides in out persistent inclination to treat creation as if it were a massive, non-negotiable zero-sum game. A zero-sum game describes the kind of interaction in which only one party can win; my victory *requires* your loss. Sports or board games are the archetypes here. Either Rafael Nadal or Novak Djokovic wins the Wimbledon final. Either IBM's Deep Blue or Garry Kasparov wins at chess. Either Google's DeepMind AlphaGo or China's Ke Jie wins Go. As with tennis, chess and Go, all too often with life – you and I can compete for food, for resources, for promotion, for space, for sexual partners, for power, for recognition or for anything else you care to mention. My success, or my country's, or my ethnic group's or my religion's is not compatible with yours, and if it's either you or me, I'm going to make damn sure it's me.

There is an alternative, however. A non-zero sum game is, predictably, the opposite, an encounter in which both parties can walk away better off. The archetype here is the famous "prisoner's dilemma" (from which so much game theory derives) in which two accused individuals can both reduce their sentences if both choose to collaborate. Trade is the archetype from real life, our exchange of goods, products, services or money benefiting us both (in theory). More mundanely, a conversation is, again in theory, the perfect example of a non-zero sum game, what you share with me enriches my life, and vice versa.

The "in theory" point is critical, however. Because rarely is life like a game of chess or a prisoner's dilemma, and most situations balance on the knife edge of being zero-sum or non-zero sum. Classic zero-sum situations, such as resource scarcity, can be turned into non-zero ones if, for example, there is a concerted effort to communicate, cooperate, share and forgive with self-discipline (as the work of economist Elinor Ostrom on the protection of the common showed with reams of supporting evidence). Even the most obvious and most serious zero-sum games, such as outright war, can be ameliorated into a more non-zero result if, for example, there is a concerted effort to rebuild states and rehabilitate relationships after a defeat (as happened after the Second World War) as opposed to punish and humiliate the defeated (as happened after the First World War). Rarely, outside of sports and board games, are zero sum games the final word.

Conversely, non-zero games can easily be turned into zero-sum ones, if "played" with the wrong attitude. The mutual benefits of trade can readily become bitter exploitation in the name of profit. The potential of a business to improve lives of customers, employees and business owners can be wrecked if turned into a conflict between labour and capital. Even a conversation can become a zero-sum game if you are using me for some other ends, or I am determined to talk at rather than with you, unwilling to hear or heed anything you say. Ultimately, we can choose to engage with reality as if it were a zero-sum game, or a non-zero one, and the consequences of our choice are momentous.

The way we turn one to the other, zero to non-zero, lies in a moment's surrender. It is the moment when we refuse the opportunity for vengeance, to pay back the Gentiles what they're really owned, to pay the Romans back in kind, to extract crippling reparations, to take the action that Tit-for-tat says is rightfully ours. It is the moment, instead, when we forgive, forbear, sacrifice – when we pour money into reconstruction and restoration in the belief that our common future is better served that way, and in the hope that you will not use my generosity simply to return to the antagonistic *status quo ante*. It is the moment when we don't simply grasp at the limited resources in the fear that they will run out before we get any, but we wait, with restraint and anxiety, in the hope that others will see our action and be similarly forbearing. It is, in effect, to play by the rules of a different game.

This was the revolution that Jesus Christ effected, giving all he was in the awful daring of a moment's surrender, an act of forgiveness and sacrifice that changes the game, breaks the chain of tit-for-tat gone awry, and replaces recrimination with restored relationship. His life and death, seen in the light of his resurrection, inspired a similar response in his early followers, and does so still today – although, as we all know – imperfectly. Within a very short period of time, those early followers understood his life and death as divine, God's answer to human desecration of our common moral landscape. Prudence, zero-sum calculation, tit-for-tat inevitably reassert themselves, but they can never retract the consequence of that moment. By this, and only this, we have existed.

Notes

Jesus Christ, game changer

1 Respectively: Josephus, *Wars* 2.169-74; Josephus, *Wars* 2.175-77; Luke 13.1; Philo, *Legatio*, 299-306; Josephus, *Antiquities*, 18.85-89. For a helpful discussion of this, see N. T. Wright, *The New Testament and the People of God* (London: SPCK, 1992), pp. 170-81.

Jesus and the scum of the earth

TERRY EAGLETON

Jesus Christ was almost certainly executed as a political rebel against the Roman imperial state. We know this because crucifixion was a penalty the Romans reserved almost entirely for political offences. The point of the punishment wasn't so much the agony it involved but the deterrence value, as dissidents were pinned up in public view as a grim warning to other potential agitators. Their broken bodies were turned into advertisements for the power of Rome. There was an element of mockery in this: look how pathetically powerless these would-be militants are! Crucifixion was a sign, a statement, a semiotic affair as well as a hideous form of torture.

Even so, Jesus got off fairly lightly. (I once made the mistake of saying this on BBC radio, and was the recipient for the next few months of shed loads of letters from conservative Evangelicals who promised to pray for my soul while deeply doubting that I was actually in possession of one.) Yet if Jesus really did only spend a few hours on the cross, as the New Testament records, then his fate could have been far worse. Some of those who were crucified thrashed around for days. What probably helped him on his way was the scourging he is said to have received shortly before his death. A massive loss of blood would have meant that he died more quickly.

Was Jesus really a political rebel, in the sense of an anti-Roman insurgent? Probably not, unless (as may be the case) the gospel writers are discreetly editing out a good deal of compromising evidence. It is true that quite a bit of what Jesus said might have sounded to the casual bystander like sound Zealot stuff. The Zealots, memorably satirized in Monty Python's *Life of Brian*, were underground Jewish revolutionaries who planned to bring the Roman state down by force. They were also extreme Jewish nationalists who dreamed of creating a purified, theocratic Jewish state once they had kicked out the occupying forces. In some ways, then, they were not all that far removed from Isis today – or from those Israeli settlers who harass and humiliate the Arabs they dispossessed of their land in the devout belief that they are doing God's will. The Pharisees, who were not at all as black as the Gospel writers paint them, were more or less the Zealots' theological wing. Perhaps Jesus curses the Pharisees as ferociously as he does partly to put some daylight between himself and the Zealots (see Matthew 23). Even so, the Pharisees, who were admired by most Jews for their piety and good works, have had an unjustifiably bad press. Unlike the Sadducees, they seem to have played no part in Jesus' death, despite the grossly improbable suggestion in Mark's Gospel that they wanted to have him killed because of his good works. The Gospels have it in for this particular tendency within Judaism, and we don't really know why. Certainly no Pharisee would have thought it against the Mosaic Law to do good works on the Sabbath. To see them as simply legalistic is a slur. Indeed, the idea that Judaism as a whole is about legal and external matters, and Christianity about spiritual and inward ones, is a piece of Christian anti-Semitism. In any case, Christian love has nothing to do with inwardness – with how one happens to be feeling. It is a material practice, a matter of feeding the hungry and welcoming the immigrant, not a sentiment or warm glow. How you feel about the people you help is neither here nor there. This is why the paradigmatic case of charity is the love of strangers and enemies, who are unlikely to evoke in us a surge of affection. The liberal wing of the Pharisees would probably have been sympathetic to a lot of what Jesus said, even to the point where one might classify him as a liberal Pharisee. All the same, he stands to the left of this group, not least in his declaration that no food was unclean, which would have been fighting talk even in liberal-Pharisaic circles.

There were probably Zealot militants, not all that far removed in their political outlook from the IRA, in Jesus' immediate entourage. One of his comrades, Simon, is directly referred to as a Zealot, while two others, James and John, are given a nickname ('Sons of Thunder') that might suggest Zealot sympathies. Judas Iscariot's surname may allude to his place of birth, but it could also be translated as 'dagger man', which might put him, too, among the anti-colonial insurgents. Perhaps he sold Jesus out to the occupying powers because he had expected him to be some kind of Lenin figure and was bitterly disenchanted when he turned out not to be. Even Peter, Jesus' right-hand man, carried a sword, an odd thing for a Galilean fisherman to do, and some scholars suspect that he may have had Zealot affiliations. (Peter, one may note in passing, wasn't the sharpest knife in the Galilean drawer. He is presented by the Gospel as constantly getting things wrong and making empty promises, not to speak of lying through his teeth.) The so-called thieves who were crucified alongside Jesus were almost certainly Zealots, as (probably) was Barabbas, the prisoner who was released by Pontius Pilate in Jesus' place.

When Mary visits her cousin Elizabeth while pregnant with Jesus, the gospel written by the man we call Luke puts into her mouth a triumphant chant known to the church as the Magnificat. It speaks of God having raised up the lowly and cast down the mighty, filled the poor with good things and sent the rich empty away. Some scholars believe that the words Mary is made to sing here reflect a Zealot chant. This theme of revolutionary reversal is almost a cliché of the Hebrew Scriptures: you will know Yahweh for who he is when you see the poor (or as St Paul colourfully calls them, the scum of the earth) coming to power. Yahweh, a terrorist of love rather than a middle-class liberal, is most certainly in this sense a revolutionist. The dispossessed are known to the Hebrew Scriptures as the *anawim*, and Mary herself, as an obscure young Galilean woman gratuitously favoured by God, is being presented by Luke as a representative of them.

So is her son, who is homeless, property-less, celibate, peripatetic, averse to material goods, hostile to the family (almost all the references to the family in the New Testament are resoundingly negative), a champion of the dispossessed and a thorn in the flesh of the political establishment. He is also remarkably laid back about sex, as the story of the woman of Samaria suggests. To talk to a young woman alone, without his minders present, was bad enough; to talk to a woman with a colourful sexual history was even worse; to talk to a Samarian woman, given that the Jews regarded Samarians as a dismally low form of life, was even more outrageous. In fact, there is almost nothing about sex in the Gospels, a fact which some of Jesus' sex-obsessed modern disciples seem not to have noticed.

Yahweh, in other words, is not a religious God, and has great trouble in trying to persuade his pathologically religious people of this inconvenient truth. You cannot make graven images of him because the only image of him is human flesh and blood. In the prophetic books of the Bible, he tells the Jews that he hates their burnt offerings and that their incense stinks in his nostrils (see Isaiah 1). What are they doing, he asks angrily, about welcoming the immigrants, protecting the widows and orphans and shielding the poor from the violence of the rich? Jesus himself is squarely in this Judaic tradition: it is not the pious and well-behaved who will enter the kingdom of God but those who give drink to the thirsty and visit the sick. In fact, in an extraordinarily audacious moment in the New Testament, he suggests that the riff-raff of the highways and byways will take priority in entering the kingdom over those faithful to the Mosaic Law. He himself eats with crooks and whores without first asking them to repent, in clear violation of Judaic orthodoxy.

Jesus has come to overthrow the Satanic image of God – the image of God as Patriarch, Big Daddy, Judge, Censor, Superego, Celestial Manufacturer, with whom you have to bargain your way to heaven by being exceptionally righteous and respectable. 'Satan' in Hebrew means adversary or accuser, and is really a false image of Yahweh – the image of him cultivated by those maso-chists among us who want a big nasty bastard of a God in order to be punished and thus be gratifyingly relieved of guilt, not some wimpish *Guardian*-reading deity who allows us to murder his own child without even a struggle. What on earth is the point of a God like that? In contrast to Satan, Jesus is the image of the Father as friend, comrade and lover, counsel for the defence rather than judge on the bench. He is a bearer of the scandalous news, offen-sive to the ears of the morally self-righteous everywhere, that we don't have to bargain our way to heaven because God loves us just as we are, in all our moral squalor. Morality for the New Testa-ment is not about rules and regulations (Paul describes the Law as "cursed"), and certainly not about sex, but about what Jesus calls abundance of life – namely the fraught, taxing business of learn-ing how to enjoy ourselves, how to live to the full, which for this particular document is a matter of living in and through each other. But which also, as we shall see, involves death.

All the same, it is hard to classify Jesus as a Zealot. If the Romans had really suspected him of leading a treasonable bunch of insurrectionists, they would almost certainly have rounded up his comrades after his death, which doesn't seem to have happened. Besides, Jesus apparently believed in paying taxes to the Roman state ('Render unto Caesar the things that are Caesar's. . .'), while the Zealots did not. This isn't necessarily to say that he lent his support to the imperial powers. On the contrary, the deeply obscure saying 'Render unto Caesar. . .' may be a smack at the cult of Caesar's divinity. It could mean "don't mistake your rulers for Gods, don't pay him divine homage". One can at least be fairly sure that 'Render unto Caesar the things that are Caesar's, and to God the things that are God's' doesn't mean that politics is one thing and religion another. Any such distinction is an anachronistic misreading, which the Jews of the time would probably have found unintelligible. It is only the modern age that enforces such a clear division between politics and religion. Those who listened to Jesus' sayings would have known well enough that the things that are God's include justice, mercy, emancipation, alms-giving, a devotion to the poor, bringing low the arrogance of the mighty and so on, all of which have their political implications. It didn't mean going to church. There were no churches. And Jesus' followers didn't need them anyway, since they were Jews, who worshipped, as Jews do, in the synagogue. They didn't see themselves as part of a new religion, and neither did Jesus. The commandment to keep holy the Sabbath day has nothing to do with going to church. It is about leisure, freedom and festivity – about resting after one's labour, and thus refusing to make a fetish of toil.

If Jesus wasn't a nationalist revolutionary, why then was he murdered by the state? The straight answer is that we don't really know. The accounts of his various trials provided by the Gospel are partial, confused and obscure. Maybe the Gospel writers themselves were unclear on the question. They were not, after all, eyewitnesses. Jesus was certainly not executed because he claimed to be divine. He uses the phrase 'Son of God' a few times, but that would not necessarily have been seen as objectionable. All Jews were the sons and daughters of God. Israel was collectively the Son of God. There would have been nothing necessarily blasphemous in the assertion. It might just have meant "king", with no divine connotations. Anyway, Jesus cannot have intended the phrase in a literal sense, since God is not generally considered to have testicles. For another thing, if Jesus had intended to suggest that he was divine, he would almost certainly have been stoned to death for blasphemy on the spot, which is one excellent reason why he makes no such unequivocal declaration. Only on a few occasions, and then mostly ambiguously, does he seem to endorse the title of the Christ. In general, however, he is notably wary of being labelled, giving the slip to the various categories that others try to foist on him. He sometimes talks of the 'Son of Man', but this is pretty obscure as well. It isn't even always clear whether he is referring to himself or someone else when he uses the title, or referring to himself under the guise of referring to someone else. The Son of Man is a shadowy figure in the Book of Daniel, but in Aramaic, the language of Jesus, it can also just be a circumlocutionary way of indicating oneself in order to avoid repeating the first person pronoun, as with the English phrase 'yours truly'. And nobody ever got strung up for that.

It seems almost certain that Jesus doesn't present himself as the Davidic Messiah, the military chieftain who would lead the Jewish people to a triumphant victory over their enemies. For one thing, the exclusively Judaic idea of Messiah would have made no sense to any but Jewish Christians. Greek Christians and others would have found it unintelligible. For another thing, the Messiah wasn't seen as the saviour of humankind – the Jews had no interest in that, being an intensely parochial bunch – but a purely local Jewish figure, a kind of Che Guavara type. He was a secular figure, not a holy man like Jesus. Besides, even if Jesus had called himself the Messiah, it would not necessarily have been blasphemous to do so. The Messiah was supposed to spring from the house of David, which is why Jesus is supposedly born in Bethlehem, the city of David. In fact, he was probably born in Nazareth. The Gospel of Luke transports him from Nazareth to Bethlehem by the narrative device of a Roman census, in which everyone had to return to where they were born in order to be counted. This seems a remarkably silly way of conducting a census. Why not just count people where they are? Besides, if there had been such an event, the whole of the Roman Empire would have been gridlocked from one end to another, and we would almost certainly know about this from secular sources, which we don't. There is no historical record of such an event. There was a Roman census a few years later, but it was confined to one part of the country only.

In any case, Messiahs don't get themselves crucified. The idea of a crucified Messiah would have struck the Jews of the time as an unspeakable moral obscenity. (The same goes for Jesus' command to let the dead bury their dead – a brutal, frightful thing to say to a people for whom burying the dead was a sacred duty). Instead, Jesus appears to go out of his way to undercut the ardent expectations of his followers. While some of them are probably anticipating a victorious march on the Jewish capital, Jesus enters Jerusalem on the back of a donkey, in a deliberately satirical, deflationary, carnivalesque gesture. He is a sick joke of a Messiah, one whose actions constitute a satirical commentary on the nature of political power as such. The power he himself represents is the only authentic and enduring one – the strength that springs from a solidarity with breakdown and failure, from a compact with the non-being and self-dispossession which is the *anawim*. When John's Gospel speaks darkly of 'the powers of this world', he has in mind the kind of violent, corrupt regime which did Jesus to death, regimes which in our own time have been busy burning Arab children in the name of freedom and democracy.

It is doubtful that either the Romans or the Sanhedrin, the Jewish ruling caste, actually suspected Jesus of seditious intentions. He had probably visited Jerusalem several times before, though the New Testament doesn't tell us so, and no move seems to have been made against him by the authorities. In any case, how was this tiny gang of illiterate, peripatetic peasants and fishermen to overthrow the mightiest state on earth? It might, however, have been politically convenient for the ruling powers to pretend that he had subversive aims. Jesus came up to Jerusalem at the time of Passover (the feast which celebrates the story of his people's emancipation from slavery in Egypt) and the political atmosphere in the capital was probably electric. A lot of people would have been looking to Jesus to do something, which he did – but according to the Gospels, it was resurrection, not insurrection. Freedom from the Egyptians would have brought to mind freedom from the Romans, and there would have been the usual assortment of minor prophets, weirdos, visionaries, hippies, con men, apocalypticists, half-baked holy men and other such flamboyant John the Baptist types knocking around the city. The place probably looked something like Woodstock. Aware of Jesus' enormous popularity with the masses, the Jewish chief priests might well have feared that his presence in the city could trigger an uprising. This might bring the full force of Roman power down on the backs of their hapless people, and so they made a pre-emptive move against him. Such an insurrection happened forty years later, when a bunch of madcap Zealot adventurists made their strike against the Romans with catastrophic consequences for the Jews, leaving the Temple in ruins. The Sanhedrin may have had Jesus killed because they were out to prevent such a disaster. On the other hand, it does not seem that their interviews of Jesus were conspicuously stacked against him.

As proof of his disruptive intent, the priests might well have appealed to the fracas in the Temple, when Jesus overturned the tables of the money changers and drove them out of the place. This was not some anti-commercial gesture. Jesus would have known well enough that those who came to the Temple to sacrifice animals might have their offering rejected as impure by the priests, and would consequently need to buy another sacrificial beast on the spot. For this, they might need to change their local currency into the metropolitan one. Hence the need for animal traders and money changers. Jesus' objection would not have been to this, but perhaps to the fact that the sacrificial tributes which people then offered were not really their own. Instead, they were part of a lucrative trade which enriched the clerical authorities, and this seems to have been enough to rouse Jesus' plebeian fury. He also shows a potentially blasphemous disrespect for the Temple by claiming that it will be replaced by his own flesh and blood. Since the Temple was among other things the seat of Jewish collaboration with the imperial forces, this kind of talk would have been potent political stuff. He is talking, incidentally, about a complex of buildings that was about the size of twelve modern football pitches, and he prophesies that not one stone will be left on another (which as the archaeologists are aware turned out not to be literally true). He is striking at the whole apparatus of priestly power, which may well have been enough to get him arrested. An assault on the temple was tantamount to an assault on God.

It would not, however, have been enough to get him executed. The right to execute was reserved by the Romans, who would have taken no interest in the esoteric theological squabbles of their colonial underlings. It was no concern to them whether an obscure, itinerant country bumpkin from provincial Galilee had delusions of divine grandeur. The country was positively stuffed with religious cranks and fanatics. They would most certainly have been alarmed, however, had Jesus been reported to them as a political threat, and it is probably this that the Sanhedrin decided to do. In a shabby political manoeuvre, then, Jesus may have been sent to his death as a political agitator or Messianic pretender without either the Jews or the Romans actually crediting the charge. It was simply expedient to get him out of the way. The sign pinned above his cross – "Jesus of Nazareth, King of the Jews", can be read among other things as a well-calculated sneer. It may be a kind of black joke, a piece of bathos on the lines of "Fred Smith of Barnsley, President of the Universe". "Galilee" was a joke to the sophisticated Jerusalem set, as the Irish are to some in the UK and the Newfoundlanders to some in the rest of Canada.

The New Testament presents the Roman governor Pontius Pilate as a vacillating, well-meaning, rather spineless liberal with a metaphysical turn of mind ('What is truth?' he inquires of Jesus). This, however, is a flagrant falsification. We happen to know something of the historical Pilate, enough to be sure that he was a ruthless despot who murdered prisoners, executed at the drop of a hat, and already stood accused of bribery, cruelty and execution without trial at the time of Jesus' appearance before him. In fact, he was finally dismissed from the imperial service for dishonourable conduct. And you had to be pretty dishonourable to be sent packing by the Romans. He would certainly have executed Jesus, not to speak of his own grandmother, without a qualm, without for a moment needing to believe that he was guilty. For their own political purposes, however, the Gospel writers are out to shift the blame for Jesus' death away from the Romans and on to the Jews. They are cosying up to the powers that be, with an eye to the early church's survival within the Roman Empire. Jesus himself refuses to assign blame to his killers and appeals instead to the notion of false consciousness to let them off the hook: 'Father, forgive them for they know not what they do.' (Luke 23.34)

The Christian belief is that crucifixion isn't quite the last word. However dire the circumstances, the power that springs from self-dispossession will win out in the end – indeed, in some mysterious way, has won out in principle already. In Christian doctrine, this is known as the resurrection. Jesus' comrades were so convinced that Calvary was not the last word that some of them were prepared to go to their own deaths for this conviction. That Jesus has risen from the dead is first reported by women, who were not regarded by the ancient Jews as acceptable witnesses. In fact, their testimony was regarded as worthless. It is second-class citizens who are first granted this revelation. On the so-called principle of embarrassment – namely, that anything the Gospel writers include which they would probably have preferred not to, but was too well attested to leave out, this is almost certainly true. The body which the various witnesses saw, however, was still marked by the wounds of crucifixion, to signify that there is no transformed existence without voyaging all the way through self- dispossession in the hope (but with absolutely no guarantees) of emerging somewhere on the other side. This is known as faith. Like much tragedy, the narrative of crucifixion and resurrection signifies that there can be no remaking without a prior breaking, a case that has political implications. Or, as W. B. Yeats more memorably put it, 'Nothing can be sole or whole / That has not been rent'. One has to live one's death to the end. If Jesus had said to himself on the cross, 'Oh well, just a few hours hanging up here, then three days in the tomb and then off to paradise for all eternity', he most certainly would not have been raised from the dead.

In the end, Jesus was killed because he spoke out fearlessly for love and justice in a political world that finds such things deeply threatening. He was, in short, a martyr, one who gives up his life as a precious gift to others, like Martin Luther King or Steve Biko. A martyr, unlike a suicide, doesn't want to die, which is perhaps why Jesus is portrayed as agonizing in the Garden of Gethsemane. It was because he was prepared to let himself go, with no thought of recompense or return, that according to the doctrine of the resurrection Jesus was so profusely rewarded. As the New Testament puts it, those who lose their lives shall find them, and according to the Gospel writers, those least capable of doing this are the rich and powerful, who cling on to themselves for dear life. If they find the self-abandonment of death difficult, it is because they have not rehearsed for it in the self-giving of their life. There are some who regard the Gospel accounts of Jesus as a source of false consolation: pie in the sky when you die, or the opium of the people – the very antithesis of revolutionary. They have clearly not taken note of the Gospels' central message: If you don't love you're dead, and if you do, they will kill you.

Christ the King
in the Fourth Gospel

A. N. WILSON

'When they had come near Jerusalem. . . Jesus sent two disciples, saying to them, "Go into the village ahead of you,
and immediately you will find a donkey tied, and a colt
with her; untie them and bring them to me. . ." This took
place to fulfill what had been spoken through the prophet,
saying,

> "Tell the daughter of Zion,
> Look, your king is coming to you,
> Humble, and mounted on a donkey. . ."'

Apart from the application of the prophecy in Zechariah (9.9),
Matthew's Gospel does not refer to Jesus as a King until Pilate,
the governor, asks him (Matt: 27.11) 'Are you the King of the
Jews?'. This is an echo of Mark 15.2 –; same episode, same
question. Mark, like Matthew, does not stress the kingship of
Jesus. Likewise, Luke 23.3 quotes from the same source that
depicts Pilate asking Jesus whether he is the King of the Jews.
For the Fourth Gospel, however, the nature of Jesus' Kingship, and of his kingdom, is central. Near the very beginning,
Nathanael proclaims, (John 1.49), 'Rabbi, you are the Son of
God! You are the King of Israel!'. His Kingship is fundamental
to how the original audience of the Gospel – in all likelihood
converted Palestinian Jews of the late first century – understand Jesus.

After the miracle of the loaves in John 6, 'Jesus realized that they were about to come and take him by force to make him king'. (John 6.15). During the triumphal entry into Jerusalem before the Passion, the crowds do not merely quote the prophetic utterance of Zechariah, already quoted, they also add, 'Blessed is the one who comes in the name of the Lord – the King of Israel'. (John 12.13). During Jesus' interrogation by Pilate, the nature of Jesus' Kingship is teased out much more fully, much more mysteriously, than in the other Gospel accounts. When the sentence is passed, Pilate says to the Jews, 'Here is your King', (John 19.14) and when they insist upon the death sentence, he asks, 'Shall I crucify your king?'(John 19.15) With one of the ironies with which this narrative bristles, Pilate writes the superscription for the cross – 'Jesus of Nazareth, the King of the Jews', and in spite of their protestations, he won't alter it. 'What I have written, I have written'. (John 19.22)

The revolutionary nature of this Gospel and the revolutionary nature of its view of Jesus, and of Kingship, are thereby emphasized. If, as seems probable, the story of Jesus' sayings, mighty deeds and signs, have been deliberately arranged to mirror the readings from the Synagogue Lectionaries; and if the life, death, and resurrection of Jesus are seen, not merely as the new Gospel, but as the ultimate revelation of the old Scriptures' meaning, then this is indeed revolutionary.

Dietary laws and circumcision marked out the Jews as different from the rest of the human race, but, as Paul and the Jesus of the first three Gospels are always ready to remind their hearers, these things are merely details. They are means to an end: they are reminders of the covenant, the great shekinah, the revelations, the promise to Abraham, the giving of the Torah to Moses, the continued speaking of the Holy Spirit through the prophets. At the heart of this Jewish distinctiveness, this setting of them apart from the Gentiles, is the tradition which tells them they have no king but God.

The folktale/mythology (call it what you will) of Samuel and Saul in 1 Samuel 8 is absolutely central to all this. In the prophet's weakened old age:

> the Lord said to Samuel, "Listen to the voice of the people in all that they say to you; for they have not rejected you, but they have rejected me from being king over them. Just as they have done to me, from the day I brought them up out of Egypt to this day, forsaking me and serving other gods."

From this moment onwards, there commences the tension that continues into the New Testament: the everlasting tension between kings and prophets. No reader of the Bible could suppose that it represents a monarchist mythology. It is the opposite. It is a story about people who know that their only King is God, by recognizing the moral law written in their hearts (Jeremiah 31.33). Paradoxically, it is David – the most loveable, inspired, flawed and memorable of all the kings of the Jews – who, in the Psalms which tradition has ascribed to him, constantly reiterates what every Jew knows to be true, namely that they have only one King: 'The Lord is King for ever and ever' (Ps.10:16); 'Who is the King of glory? The Lord of . . . hosts' (Ps 24:10). 'God is the King of all the earth' (Ps 47:7), etc.

In all four Gospels, Jesus reiterates that, whereas the Gentiles exercise lordship (Mark 10.42, Luke 22.25, etc.) as kings, it shall not be so among his followers. This is one of the most revolutionary, if not *the* most revolutionary, assertion in the entire New Testament, a complete reversal of the notion of hierarchy upon which, hitherto, certainly in the societies of the Mediterranean, civilization itself had been founded. Jesus speaks in the tradition of the Hebrew prophets, and then, in the developed Christology of the Fourth Gospel, he speaks as more than a prophet. He speaks (passim) as the EGO EIMI, the I AM who had spoken to Moses, as the Word Made Flesh (John 1:14).

Since the conversion of Constantine and the adoption of Christianity as the religion of the Empire, it has been natural for Christians to try either to ignore this central message of the Gospel or to twist and mould it to suggest that there might be such a thing as a Christian society, or a Christian view of politics. Christians have tried, as Malcolm Muggeridge used to say, to make Jesus into the Honourable Member for Galilee South: an essentially sensible person who believed in a decent ordering of the *polis*. Such distortion, or deliberate ignoring, of the message of the Bible in general, and of the Fourth Gospel in particular, has led to many of the reforms and changes to society of which Christians are most proud – chief of which, in the last two centuries, is probably the abolition of slavery, partly as the result of campaigns by evangelical Christians such as William Wilberforce.

There is a reason why the world waited 1800 years after the King of the Jews died a slave's death, before it became a Christian orthodoxy to abolish slavery. The New Testament preaches the much more revolutionary doctrine, namely that we should all aspire to the condition of slaves, not that the institution of slavery should be abolished. Whereas many Christians today consider that the abolition of slavery in the nineteenth century was a wonderful triumph of 'Christian' values over cruel and wicked men, we can see that it came at a time when Christianity itself was beginning its process of unravelling. Many of the abolitionists were not evangelical Christians, but unbelievers, and there is no coincidence in the fact that the human race chose to abolish slavery at the time when so many intellectuals in Europe and America had taken leave, in part, or entirely, of belief in orthodox Christianity. Not that orthodoxy, with a small or a big 'O', had ever been able to absorb – who could? – the revolutionary import of what the King, in the Fourth Gospel, was saying. Whereas the Orthodox Church canonized the Emperor Constantine, and keeps his feast day on 21 May, the New Testament Christ told Pilate, 'My kingdom is not from this world. If my kingdom were from this world, my followers would be fighting to keep me from being handed over to the Jews. But as it is, my kingdom is not from here'. (John18.36) The pacifism that was practised by early Christians until the conversion of Constantine was one of the key features which distinguished them from those 'from this world'. When Tolstoy, in the late nineteenth century, reminded the world of this doctrine (in such key works as *The Kingdom of God is Within You*), it was not surprising that the Russian Orthodox Church excommunicated him – not least because he airily chose, in his rewriting of the New Testament, to excise all references to Christ's miracles, and indeed to a belief in the Resurrection itself. In his way, he was as guilty as the Orthodox censors of trying to rewrite the Bible to fit it into his own vision of the world, rather than allowing its revolutionary message to transform *him*.

In the Apocalypse, or book of Revelation, written in the tradition of Jewish Apocalyptic writings at the end of the first century, we see, in the most advanced state, an attitude toward the human *polis,* which is surely there in embryo in all four Gospels and in the fourth in particular: namely, an absolute distrust of the human city, of human political institutions, of trade, of art, architecture, marriage and giving in marriage, and all the institutions which human beings have traditionally regarded as civilized. The visionary of Patmos hates 'the merchants of the earth' (Rev. 18.3) and those who trade in cargoes of 'costly wood, bronze, iron, and marble, cinnamon, spice, incense, myrrh, frankincense, wine, olive oil, choice flour and wheat, cattle and sheep, horses and chariots'. (Rev. 18.11) Clothes, jewels, ships and seafarers, musicians and architects are all, literally, going to go up in smoke in the great and final judgement. (Rev. 18 and 19 passim). The absolute distrust, not merely of the power of Rome, but, by implication, of all human institutions, artifacts, diversions and pleasures implied in the last book of the Christian Bible is 'revolutionary' indeed.

Aeschylus (c. 525 BCE-456 BCE), four and half centuries before Christ, and, presumably, some five centuries before the Apocalypse of John, reworked, in *Prometheus Bound*, a myth which is, as it were, naturalistic, rational. It depicts the Titan, Prometheus, being punished for having introduced fire to the human race, and, by extension, having taught them the arts of civilization. . .

> They were like children in their wits before,
> Until I taught them how to use their minds. . ..
> They knew no brick-built houses
> To shield them from the sun, nor works of wood;
> Like crawling ants they hid themselves in holes. . ..
> (translation Prometheus Unbound, 45ff. James Room in
> *The Greek Plays*, Modern Library, New York, 2016)

Aeschylus and the New Testament seem agreed that there is a gulf fixed between the activities of the *polis* and the heavenly wisdom: that God and civilization are at odds. It is difficult for us, given the Miltonic reworkings of this myth in English – making Satan a Promethean figure, and Shelley reworking Milton *and* Aeschylus to give us his Romantic Age revolutionary *Prometheus Unbound*, not to read back into the old Greek mythology something of the modern atheism. But there is, surely, inherent in the story, the notion that the human race will one day outgrow Zeus and authoritarian religion and learn to live by its own ingenuity, its own political and ethical systems. This is why the Aeschylean Prometheus is chained to his rock until the God-Man, descendant of Zeus and the cow-maiden Io, Herakles, will in the future come to rescue him.

Clearly, any Christian reading, even more seeing, of the drama of the suffering Titan Prometheus, thinks inevitably of the cross of Jesus, and the suffering of the Man-God for the redemption of all humanity. Here the Fourth Gospel is more specific in its theology than any of the synoptics. 'And just as Moses lifted up the serpent in the wilderness, so must the Son of Man be lifted up, that whoever believes in him may have eternal life.' (John 3.14)

The Fourth Gospel comes much closer than the other Gospels to a 'mythological' depiction of Jesus. On one level, it comes much closer to the Promethean idea that, after obedience to a purely 'divine' origin of skills or ethics, these gifts have now passed into human hands. Whereas, however, the Greeks learned from Aeschylus that a generous Titan, Prometheus, is chained to a rock in order to give them moral and political autonomy, the followers of Jesus, who is nailed to a tree in order to grant them everlasting life, can only come to the Father through him. They cannot, in the phrase that was common during the 1960s and the days of 'Death of God' theology, 'take leave of God'. On the contrary: the Greeks, liberated by Prometheus, can build cities, philosophies, dramas, sculptures, and ethical systems. The followers of Jesus, in contrast, will by a supreme paradox, enjoy the blessing offered by the deceitful serpent in the Garden of Eden. They will discern the will and mind of God; they will know the true Good, but only by accepting that Jesus and the Father are one, that, although no man has seen God at any time, he is revealed, in his glory and fullness, in Jesus.

And the kingdom of which the Christians become citizens is not from (or of) this world. It is absolutely at variance with this world. Christians, by embracing the faith of Jesus, are true revolutionaries, because they are not to be regarded as citizens of this world at all. Their only king is God, or the Son in whom the will of the Father is made manifest, the Son in whose death and Resurrection the Father is truly glorified. Prometheus gives men and women the chance to develop human civil+ization, to live an independent adult life. Christ the King, in the Fourth Gospel, gives Christians the chance to adopt, even while living bodily on this planet, the values of God alone.

Ever since God spoke to Samuel and suggested that *faute de mieux* – the old prophet must choose a King, since 'they have rejected me from being king over them' (1 Samuel 8.7) – the Jews had carried, within their self-identifying mythology, the creative tension between their God and their desire to be like all the other nations of the earth, with kings, hierarchies, artifacts, visual arts, etc. Their prophets repeatedly called them back to realize the essential incompatibility between the ways of God and the ways of what the Fourth Gospel calls the *kosmos*.

In the books of the Maccabees, written in the first century BCE for Alexandrian Jews, we read about the persecutions and threats to Judaism under Anthiochus IV (175 BCE) and the rebellion of Judas Maccabeus (i.e. the 'hammerlike') to defend the Temple and cleanse it of non-Jewish cultic activity. There was a constant fear, in the centuries from this time onwards until the catastrophic sack of Jerusalem in 70 CE, that the Gentiles – Ptolemy – Seleucids – Romans – would defile the Temple, destroy Judaism, or force Jews to compromise their faith. Since all the Gospels in some way or another allude to the destruction of the Temple, it would seem probable that they post-date this event. But even if you believe that they are, in fact, prophecies, which pre-date the disaster, the point is the same: Jesus is the New Temple. When he spoke of the destruction of the old Temple, he spoke of his own body, and when he spoke of its rebuilding, he spoke of his resurrection. But he was not, clearly, returning to earth in his resurrection to start a new 'civilization'. The figure encountered on the shore of the Sea of Galilee, cooking a fish breakfast and calling Simon Peter to feed his lambs, was, we must assume, preparing the disciples for the end of time. All the other New Testament writers, from Paul, writing in the 50s, to the seer of Patmos, writing at the end of the century, are looking forward to a world that which is soon going to pass away.

There cannot be a more 'revolutionary' vision of the world than the supposition that it is about to come to its end, to be replaced with a rule of the saints, or a New Jerusalem. There is, for all the New Testament writers, a complete divide between the Caesars, with their laws, armies, aqueducts and cities, and the new kingdom for which the early church prayed every time it used the words it attributed to its Divine Lord and King: *Thy kingdom come.*

This is what makes the Passion drama in the Fourth Gospel so devastating, so shocking. For when Pilate asks the Jews (perhaps "Judaizers" or "Judaoi" is a more accurate way of writing, especially if the original "church" for which the Gospel was written were themselves Jewish converts) 'Shall I crucify your king?' they reply, 'We have no king but the emperor.' (John 19.15) In other words, the enemies of Christ, in the Fourth Gospel, have abandoned all that was revolutionary, all that was distinctive, all that was interesting, and all that was Jewish about Judaism. They have capitulated. The crowds, in Chapter 6, who wanted to make Jesus into a King, had wanted him to become another

Judas Maccabeus, a warrior-king fighting the Roman legions. They mistook his purpose, his identity, but their heart was in the right place. The Sanhedrin, and the High Priests before Pilate, have gone over to the dark side: they have no king except Caesar – that is, in terms of the Apocalypse, the Great Beast, whose mark is 666.

The question for the modern reader, presumably, is what are we meant to make of all this? That is to say, can we hope to read the Fourth Gospel and become followers of its King? Or must we merely read it as a document of the greatest historical interest, but which can in no way be absorbed into a twenty-first century soul or heart. After all, 1900 years or more have passed since the author of that Gospel laid down his pen (or their pens, if you believe in some form of multiple authorship), and since the early church or churches realized that the Parousia, the coming of the Lord on the clouds first foretold to the Thessalonians by Paul, before the descent of the new Jerusalem foreseen in Revelation, was not going to happen in their lifetimes.

Allusion has already been made in this essay to the claim by the evangelical Christians of the eighteenth and early nineteenth centuries that the kingdom had been advanced by abolition. There is no doubt that abolition was good news for the slaves. It was good news for the human race. It was less good news for Christian exegesis. It is so easy, and so wrong, to translate New Testament ethics into a mere striving after niceness or the improvement of society. The world would be a much better place if we could all contrive to be kinder to one another, and if we could find ways to be nicer people. These words of mine, however, which could be said to summarize the modern attitude to life (secular and Christian, since the beginning of the nineteenth century) are not the everlasting Gospel, and are not the revolutionary Gospel of Christ the King as expressed in the

Fourth Gospel – the most eloquent, finished, and disturbing of all the four Gospels.

Indeed, one must go further than this and say that the pursuit of social virtue plays no part at all, as far as one can see, in the Gospel. No one in the pages of the Fourth Gospel, or of the Synoptics, calls for better living conditions for the Galilean villagers, better education for the Palestinian children, improvements in diet or medicinal supplies for the poorer parts of Jerusalem, or indeed for any of the things which would immediately occur to the visitor to such utterly deprived areas from the nineteenth, twentieth or twenty-first centuries.

If the Gospel is "revolutionary", it is decidedly not "revolutionary" in the post-French Revolutionary sense of that word. Neither liberty, equality, nor fraternity play any part in the ethics of the New Testament, and, as we have already stated, the poor and the slaves come before us, not as objects of pity but as role models. Yet, the Fourth Gospel, more than others, also suggests, paradoxically, that the central characters are, if not rich, then persons of some substance. The disciple whom Jesus loved has an entrée into the High Priest's house, and the word used for the fish, during the great miracle of the loaves – *opsarion* – is a trade word, reminding us of the tradition that the apostles were fishermen, who sold their catch, and perhaps had a contract to sell as it were wholesale to the greater households of Jerusalem. The miraculous draught of fishes, which in the Fourth Gospel occurs at the end, and is undoubtedly in part as a symbol or metaphor of the burgeoning and growing church, occurs to fishermen who are clearly engaged in a profit-making trade, and they have a boat which is large enough to accommodate a huge catch. Moreover, in this Gospel, we have, not merely the witness of Joseph of Arimathea who takes the body of Jesus for burial, but also of Nicodemus, the member of the Council or Sanhedrin, clearly an establishment-figure who, in coming to Jesus "by night" is representative of observant Jewry still, at that early stage of the narrative, in darkness. (Later, he will come to the light as Judas steps out into the night of betrayal and damnation).

So, the revolutionary nature of the Gospel, if it exists, is not what, from the 1960s onwards, was called the "social Gospel". Indeed, there is no social Gospel since Jesus and his followers in this version of the story are not merely non-social but antisocial, in the sense of seeing no future for the *polis*, no future for the human race, as such, except for those who believe on the name of the Lord Jesus and inherit "eternal life".

The revolution, which a reading of the Fourth Gospel would cause in a reader of the twenty-first century would, therefore, be a revolution of the inward person, rather than of society. It would presumably occur when the reader identified with the various characters who are brought to meet the Lord in the course of the first eleven chapters – Nathaniel who was seen by Jesus under the fig tree – at first sceptical that any good could come out of Nazareth, and then converted to the view that he was the Chosen, the Anointed One; Nicodemus, coming by night; the Samaritan woman by the well, who finds in Jesus one who can see into her very soul and tell her everything about her life; the lame man who cannot reach the waters of Bethesda in time to be healed; the blind man in Jericho. We are supposed to be all these people, culminating in the one whom Jesus loved, who is actually brought back from the grave in Chapter 11.

The narrative tells us that Jesus loved Lazarus, wept at his death and brought him back to life. In the second half of the story, after this stupendous miracle, the most dramatic miracle story in the whole New Testament, Lazarus is unnamed, but is it not likely that he is also meant, when the unnamed "disciple whom Jesus loved" is mentioned – especially when we learn in the final chapter of the book that a rumour has gone round the early church that this disciple would never die? It would be an odd story to tell about an ordinary mortal. If one had been brought back from the dead, however, it would be only natural to suppose that he would be, if not immortal, at least given a special lease of life until the coming of the Lord on the last day.

The raising of Lazarus is plainly meant to be taken literally, as are the stories of the Resurrection appearances of Jesus. Doubting Thomas, who kneels before the risen Lord, and exclaims, 'My Lord and my God' is the most vivid and the most intimate of all the semi-symbolic figures, who are intended both as distinct figures in an historical narrative and figures with whom the hearer/reader is intended to identify. The nature of the "revolution", for the modern reader of the Fourth Gospel must therefore be that we hear the story, or read the story, as sceptics in the first place, but as those who come to believe in 'life eternal', as a literal reality. (Most readers or hearers, in this century or any other, would, naturally enough, be inclined, like the Athenians who heard the preaching of Paul of Tarsus, to turn away sceptically when the Resurrection of the body is mentioned.)

The Fourth Gospel asserts that it was written, 'so that you may come to believe that Jesus is the Messiah, the Son of God, and that through believing you may have life in his name'. (John 20.31) There can be no greater revolution in a person's life than to make this realization, for it is to make two discoveries at once. First, it is to discover Christ's power to save each and every human soul who turns to him in faith. Second, it is to recognize that the kingdom he came to establish does, in fact, exist upon earth. This, surely, is the clue to the great sixth chapter of the Gospel when the crowds, after the miraculous feeding, come and try to 'take him by force to make him king'. (John 6.15) Had this been his mission, and had he accepted the wish of the crowd, he would have been a great Jewish hero in the tradition of Judas Maccabeus. He would not, however, have been what this Gospel says he was, the Word of God, coming to establish a kingdom 'not of this world'.

After the long discourse about the mystery of the bread, in which he tells his followers that he himself is the Bread of Life, that those who would have eternal life are those who eat his flesh and drink his blood, we are told that many of his followers deserted him. It was too revolutionary to bear, or to hear. There is one, Simon Peter, to whom Jesus turned. Simon Peter is asked why he, too, does not desert Jesus, and he replies, 'Lord, to whom shall we go? You have the words of eternal life'. (John 6.68) It is this Simon Peter who denies Christ three times at the time of his trial. (John 18.27) Nevertheless, it is this same Peter who, at the end of the Gospels, is chosen as his representative among the Twelve, the head of his earthly Church.

The Gospel is written after Peter's martyrdom for the faith (John 6.23), but there can be no doubt of the Gospel's revolutionary intention – which is that the kingdom that is 'not of this world' should be understood as those belonging to the eucharistic society of the sixth chapter – all of whom are united, according to Christ's prayer in Gethsemane, with Jesus and the Father: 'I have given them your word, and the world has hated them because they do not belong to the world' (John 17.16). Their head on earth is Peter, and his successors, human, weak, and capable of denying Christ in their own human persons, but in so far as they hold together the unbroken and unbreakable eucharistic unity, custodians of Christ's revolutionary institution, the Church. St Peter and the apostles are therefore the earthly representatives of a kingdom that is eternal.

In 1925, in his encyclical *Quas Primas*, Pope Pius XI instituted the Feast of Christ the King as the conclusion of the liturgical year: 'It was surely right, then, in view of the common teaching of the sacred books, that the Catholic Church, which is the kingdom of Christ on earth, destined to be spread among all men and all nations, should with every token of veneration salute her Author and Founder in her annual liturgy as King and Lord, and as King of Kings.'

Worshippers of revolution: Islamic perspectives on Jesus

TARIF KHALIDI

On April 8, 2018, the Secretary-General of the Lebanese party Hizbullah, al-Sayyid Hasan Nasrullah, delivered a speech, which included the following passage:

> Ours is a culture of hope, hope in the fulfilment of God's promise and in the future: a future that is near, intermediate or distant; hope in that which is to come and from which we are separated by a time unknown to us; hope in the return of Christ the Messiah to this world in order to drive out all thieves from all temples and to establish the Kingdom of God; hope in the appearance of a descendant of Muhammad who would establish justice, security and peace throughout the earth.

Who did Nasrullah have in his sights in that speech, and why did he evoke that startling messianic longing for the Second Coming of Christ? Nasrullah had in mind the kleptocratic political class in Lebanon, and as a Muslim Shi`ite cleric and resistance leader with a massive following throughout the Arabic and Islamic world, he was referring to a fairly widespread Muslim hope for the coming of an era of universal justice and peace, to be ushered in by Christ's second coming and then by the Muslim Mahdi, or Messiah.

In order to understand the full range of these messianic expectations, it would be useful to cast our eyes at how Jesus has been perceived by Islam across the centuries. For Islamic literature, sacred, pious and profane, and both pre-modern and modern, contains what is without doubt the largest and richest volume of Jesus stories and sayings, as well as poems and other literary and theological writings that relate to him, to be found outside the Christian tradition.

This range of Muslim perceptions of Jesus may be divided into four overlapping historical periods:

1 Jesus reconfigured as a Muslim prophet
2 Jesus as 'Prophet of the Heart'
3 Jesus between east and west
4 Jesus the revolutionary

I propose to examine each of these periods in turn, though the last period will, given the principal theme of this work, receive the largest attention.

1. Jesus reconfigured as a Muslim prophet

In the first period, Jesus makes his entry into the Muslim tradition through the Qur'an and the *Hadith,* i.e. the exemplary sayings and actions of Muhammad. In the Qur'an, and to summarize what is in essence a mixed bag of images, Jesus is reconfigured as a Muslim prophet. Called consistently 'Jesus son of Mary', arguably to emphasize his immaculate and miraculous birth, he is nevertheless "cleansed" from the "legends" that surround him among his Christian followers, foremost among which are his incarnation and crucifixion. Reduced to the status of a human prophet, like all other Qur'anic prophets, a status that Jesus is humbly made to accept and humbly to deny that he ever preached a triune god, he is nevertheless singled out from among these prophets by being called the 'Spirit of God' and a 'Word from Him', epithets unique to him. There is no ministry and no Passion. Instead, the Qur'an tilts back to his wondrous birth and his miracles and affirms that what it says about him is the historical "truth" (*al-haqq*). He is further honoured by being the prophet who announced the coming of Muhammad. But no other Qur'anic prophet is subjected to the same reconfiguring process, and Jesus emerges from the Qur'an in a new and emphatically human garb where he explicitly denies his divinity, while his crucifixion is described as an illusion, as was done by some early Christian gnostic gospels.

But once this new and "cleansed" Jesus is in place, it appears as if the Qur'an, having won its argument against the "fabrications" of his followers, treats him and them with exceptional tenderness. God, in addition to the many divine favours he granted him, fortifies Jesus with the 'Holy Spirit' and 'Wisdom' and reveals the 'Evangel' to him, planting kindness and compassion in the hearts of those who follow him. Rejecting his passion and crucifixion, the Qur'an substitutes for them his ascension while still alive, leading to the elaboration of this event in the *Hadith* and creeds. With regard to his followers, while the Qur'an expresses an often violent opposition to trinitarianism, it nevertheless describes them as 'the nearest in amity' to the Muslims 'because among them are priests and monks, and they do not grow proud.'

These images of Jesus and his followers in the Qur'an are somewhat discordant and may well reflect Muhammad's checkered encounters with the Christian communities of his time and place.

The *Hadith*, reflecting the piety of the first two Islamic centuries, most of which was in circulation and in written form in the late ninth and early tenth centuries A.D. picks up on some of the Qur'anic images above, but now formally expressed in the words of Muhammad as transmitted by his pious community. The contrast with the Jesus images, described above as discordant, cannot be clearer; in *Hadith*, these images are uniformly positive. To begin with, Jesus, now fully "cleansed", is a central figure in the scenario of the end of days. He will descend from heaven as a "just ruler", judge according to both Qur'an and Evangel, perform a number of symbolic acts like breaking crosses, killing pigs and abolishing the *jizya,* or poll tax, imposed on non-Muslims possessing revealed scriptures. An era of prosperity will immediately follow where 'there will no longer be anyone to accept charity'. This reign of Jesus is said in one *hadith* to last forty years and will conclude with Jesus killing the anti-Christ (*al-Dajjal*), bringing the world to its end.

Jesus, seen by Muhammad on his Night Journey to heaven, also acquires a distinct physical appearance. He is described in *Hadith* as 'of medium height and moderate in complexion', inclined to reddish white in colour, and with 'lanky hair as if he had just come out of the bath'. So the *Hadith* now cleanses him literally, endowing him with a physical stature and colouring suggesting moral and aesthetic moderation, and implying probably more than this to early Muslims attuned to physiognomy. His immaculateness is underlined in one *hadith,* which states that all humans are touched by Satan at the moment of birth except for Jesus, whom Satan failed to touch. Among contemporaneous Muslims, he is said to most closely resemble 'Urwa ibn Mas'ud al-Thaqafi, an early Muslim convert and grandee of the town of Ta'if, near Mecca, who was shot with arrows while preaching and met a martyr's death.

There is, finally, the closeness of Jesus to Muhammad, in both kinship and prophetic time. All prophets are described in Hadith as *abna' 'allat* , brothers from the same father but from different mothers. Jesus, however, is the closest among them to Muhammad since no prophet appeared in 'the six-hundred year interval' between them, and Jesus had thus acted as Muhammad's harbinger. The closeness is further emphasized in *hadiths*, which state, for example, that whoever first believed in Jesus then in Muhammad would receive a double reward from God. In other *hadiths*, a typical Muslim confession of faith in God's unity and Muhammad's prophecy must include the assertion of the human nature of Jesus, while a believer who states that he does not know if Jesus is a prophet would be declared an infidel.

The Qur'anic Jesus is a polemical argument. The *Hadith* Jesus reflects the consensual verdict of the community. He is authoritatively enshrined in Muslim faith, a figure of the Apocalypse, a trans-historical icon, the alpha of the era of Muhammad and the omega of the world's end.

2. Jesus as "Prophet of the Heart"

The second range of Muslim perceptions of Jesus begins approximately in the eighth century and lasts until the eighteenth: a corpus of Jesus sayings and stories that began to appear in the Islamic literary tradition and circulated all the way from Spain to China. This is where educated Muslims of the pre-modern as well as the modern periods were most likely to encounter the figure of Jesus outside of the Qur'an and *Hadith*. The most recent attempt to collect these sayings unearthed some 300 of them, though their number will no doubt increase with further research. These sayings and stories are found almost everywhere in Islamic literature: in literary anthologies, in books of pious devotions and asceticism, in theological and historical works, in manuals of politics and government, in mystical works and in tales of prophets and saints. The earliest saying thus far unearthed and dating from the early eighth century, runs as follows: 'Jesus saw a man in the act of stealing and asked him: "Were you stealing?" The man answered: "Never! I swear

127

by Him than whom none is more worthy of worship." Jesus said: "I believe in God and falsify my eyes."' This somewhat cryptic saying may suggest that for Jesus faith in God overrides any sin, even when committed *in flagrante*. It may also suggest an abstention from judgement in order to preserve social peace, thus giving the thief the benefit of the doubt. Again, this exchange may have political implications: rulers should be left to God's judgement even if they are manifest sinners.

In some ways, this earliest saying foreshadows what is to come in later sayings. It dresses Jesus in Muslim garb, making him sound like some ascetic *shaykh,* who walks the streets admonishing sinners but is reluctant to judge when God's name is invoked. Could the Jesus of the Gospels have said and acted in the same way? This is what most of these sayings aim to capture, i.e. to make these sayings worthy of the revered prophet to whom they are ascribed.

When we cast our eye at that total corpus, which one might call 'the Gospel according to the Muslims', we find them divided into two or three principal groups. The first group are redactions from the Gospels, the most popular of which seems to be the Gospel according to Matthew. Thus, another early saying runs as follows: 'Jesus said: "If it is a day of fasting for one of you, let him anoint his head and beard and wipe his lips so that people will not know he is fasting. If he gives with the right hand let him hide this from his left hand. If he prays, let him pull down the door curtain for God apportions praise as he apportions livelihood."' The core of this saying comes from the Sermon on the Mount in Matthew, but the very last phrase, about God apportioning praise, seems like an addition, not entirely relevant, by an Islamic redactor. This group, i.e. sayings with a Gospel core, account for about ten per cent of the total.

The second and most interesting group of sayings includes sayings and stories from the rich heritage of Near Eastern wisdom literature, with many of them reminiscent of the ascetic pronouncements of the Desert Fathers. Thus, "Jesus owned nothing but a comb and a cup. He once saw a man combing his beard with his fingers, so Jesus threw away the comb. He saw another man drinking from a river with his hand cupped so Jesus threw away the cup." In many such sayings, Jesus is depicted as an ascetic wanderer who sternly renounces the world: 'Jesus used to say: "Truly I say to you, to eat barley bread, to drink pure water and to sleep upon dunghills with the dogs more than suffices him who wishes to inherit paradise."' Here, the Muslim redactor reveals his hand by imitating the speaking style of Jesus in the Gospels, viz. 'Truly I say to you,' but the saying is a fiercer condemnation of the world than anything in the Gospels. He is a wanderer: 'Jesus was a constant traveller in the land, never abiding in a house or village. His clothing consisted of a cloak of coarse hair and two hair shirts. When night fell, his lamp was the moonlight, his bed the earth, his pillow a stone, his food the plants of the field. He often spent whole days and nights without food.' To emphasize the transience of the world, one saying runs as follows: 'The world is a bridge. Cross this bridge but do not build upon it.' The world can be a fatal attraction as in: 'He who desires worldly things is like the man who drinks sea water: the more he drinks the more thirsty he becomes, until it kills him.'

At least half these sayings and stories depict a total renunciation of the world and an identification with the poor, which is crucial to his mission. Poverty, humility, silence and patience are the cardinal virtues, and the true believer is a sorrowing traveller, a "stranger" or "guest" in this world. To emphasize the corruption of the world, Jesus often interrogates ruined habitations or human skulls that reveal to him the treacherous delusions of existence and the transitory nature of all worldly glory.

This ascetic Jesus was to become a favourite among Muslim Sufis or ascetic mystics, who embraced him as a patron saint, a sort of Sufi *avant la lettre*. For many Sufi who contemplated the attributes of God, these attributes were divided into attributes of his beauty (*jamal*) and attributes of his awe and majesty (*jalal*). Among Sufis, Jesus was the image of God's beauty, epitomizing divine attributes like mercy, love and forgiveness.

Perhaps as much as a quarter of these sayings reveal Jesus in the garb of a teacher of compassion and good manners, and a profound reader of the human heart. Thus: 'Jesus said: "Blessed is he who sees with his heart but whose heart is not in what he sees."' Or else: 'Jesus met a man and asked him, "What are you doing?" "I am devoting myself to God," the man replied. Jesus asked, "Who is caring for you?" "My brother," replied the man. "Your brother is more devoted to God than you are."' Then again: 'Jesus and his disciples passed by a dog's carcass. The disciples said, "How foul is his stench!" Jesus said, "How white are his teeth!"' The redactor adds: 'He said this in order to teach them a lesson – namely, to forbid slander.'

A sizeable number of sayings concern scholars and their grave responsibility towards society: 'Jesus was asked: "Spirit and Word of God, who is the most seditious of men?" He replied, "The scholar who is in error. If a scholar errs, a host of people will fall into error because of him."' Or else: 'Woe to you, evil scholars! For the sake of a despicable world and a calamitous desire, you squander the kingdom of heaven and forget the terrors of the Day of Judgement.'

Where politics are concerned, Jesus is consistently a quietist, thus: 'Jesus said to his disciples: "Just as kings left wisdom to you, so you should leave the world to them."' A more explicit saying runs as follows: 'The disciples said to Jesus: "What do you say about rulers?" He answered: "They have been made into a temptation for you. Let not your love for them lead you into sinning against God, nor your hatred of them lead you out of God's obedience. If you fulfil your obligations towards them, you will escape their evil and your faith will remain intact.'" Like wealth or human glory, rulers are a "temptation" to the believer and must neither be wooed nor confronted.

One of the largest collections of these sayings and stories is found in the works of al-Ghazali (d. 1111), a towering figure of pre-modern Islamic culture. Mystic and theologian, it was he who dubbed Jesus the "Prophet of the Heart", recognizing in Jesus a figure who best exemplified his own reform programme to infuse into Islam the necessary spiritual element that he found lacking among the scholars of his day. These he accused of narrow literalism, worldly preoccupations and a petty concern with the minutiae of the law. Somewhat like Dante in the next century, and concerned to protect social peace at all costs, al-Ghazali argued for a division of authority between a Sultan, who took care of mundane affairs and a caliph, who took care of spiritual affairs. Among all the prophets of the Qur'an it was Jesus who, for Ghazali, symbolized the struggle between the letter and the spirit of the law, and who drew the sharpest line between the realm of power and the realm of the heart.

3. Jesus between east and west

The third phase in our survey is another lengthy period that accompanied the millennium-long encounter between the Muslim east and the Christian west. This is a period that began with the extraordinary Muslim conquests in the seventh century A.D. and by the middle of the eighth had created a Muslim empire stretching from Spain to the borders of China, bringing perhaps millions of Christians of various denominations under Islamic rule. The subsequent ebb and flow of these conquests need not detain us here, nor do we need to linger over the centuries of peaceful coexistence between Muslims and Christians in regions like Spain, Sicily and the Near and Middle East. All these are subjects that have received considerable scholarly attention. Instead, what I attempt here is a sketch of the figure of Jesus at certain high points of intensity during that protracted encounter, and to extend that sketch to cover the nineteenth and twentieth centuries. These periods of intensity inevitably produced a new mood of polemics where Jesus is gradually distanced from his violent and ignorant followers. This was a theme that more or less persisted all the way until modern times.

The first such moment of intensity is the series of wars against Byzantium as reflected in Arabic poetry of say the eighth to the eleventh centuries, with poetry acting as the chief purveyor of the "social imaginary" in the pre-modern period. These wars provided early Muslim poets with the chance to celebrate the exploits of Muslim heroes, and militant prophets like David and Solomon were more appropriate as exemplars of righteous wars than Jesus. Thus, for a celebrated poet like al-Farazdaq (d. 728), Jesus is a figure of purity and sanctity, invoked most often when excessive praise of some grandee is called for, e.g.

> There is no other mother than the mother of Jesus
> Who is more virtuous or noble than yours.

Or else,

> Had not Jesus heralded him and clearly indicated his (i.e. Muhammad's) name,
> It would have been you who was the prophet that called to the light.

The enemies, whether Byzantines or Crusaders, were invariably referred to as 'worshippers of the cross' or as 'polytheists', and Jesus, by and large, recedes into the background. Where, rarely, he is mentioned by name in poetry, this is almost always to compare some event, for instance, to the miracles of Jesus or to revere a ruler as 'a priest reveres Jesus'. His religion is said to have been distorted by his followers, an echo of the older Qur'anic charge that the Scriptures of Jews and Christians had been wilfully 'tampered with' in order to hide the truth of Muhammad. Thus, a poem that called upon Muslims to join forces against the Crusaders under King Louis IX, who had landed in Egypt in 1249, includes the following lines:

> *O you who claim to follow the religion of Christ,*
> *And a long argument can be adduced against such a*
> *claim,*
> *You have perverted the religion of Christ,*
> *As also the teachings of Moses and the laws of*
> *Abraham.*

The 'long argument' referred to above was of course the vast literature of polemic, in prose, that began sometime in the ninth century when Muslim scholars gained a direct knowledge of the Gospels and proceeded to quote chapter and verse in order to demonstrate that Jesus himself never claimed he was divine. This polemical literature engaged some of the most celebrated theologians of Islam, such the Qadi 'Abd al-Jabbar (d. 1025) and Ibn Taymiyya (d. 1328) and is too extensive to be dealt with here. If one wishes to summarize the thrust of these polemics one might posit that they often sound like an elaboration of the Qu'anic attempt to "cleanse" Jesus, this time from the logical and theological absurdities of his followers. One might say that, for Muslim theologians, Jesus was too central a spiritual figure to be left to the Christians.

These polemics would flare up or subside in response to external threats or internal frictions between Muslims and Christians, for the Christians living in Muslim states never ceased to play a prominent social role throughout these centuries, and were sometimes favoured as state officials by Muslim rulers who had less to fear from them as potential rivals than their own Muslim subjects. Where love of a Christian girl or youth is described, a playful reference to Christ may be invoked, as in a poem by Ibn al-Qaisarani (d. 1153) addressed to a girl called Maria:

She has a Christ-like face
With which she resurrects the dead.

Christ's resurrection would eventually become a central theme among modernist Muslim poets, as will be argued later.

One other arena of polemic concerned miracles. Here, it was found necessary by Muslim theologians not only to attribute miracles to Muhammad, in direct defiance of the Qur'an and various pronouncements by the Prophet himself, but to make his miracles greater in quantity and significance than those of earlier prophets. In a work called *Proofs of Prophecy*, the celebrated Hadith scholar and theologian Abu Nu'aim al-Isfahani (d. 1038) passes from prophet to prophet but is aware of the fact that the miracles of Jesus are the most widely known among the Muslim community, and thus the most challenging to emulate or surpass. As he lists the miracles in the Gospels, viz. Jesus' virginal conception, his curing of the blind and leprous, the raising of the dead, knowledge of the Unseen, his ascetical life and travels, and his ascent to heaven, Abu Nu'aim cites reports where Muhammad outperforms Jesus in every department.

This triumphalist tone accompanied a second wave of Muslim conquests in Europe, which began in the eleventh century and lasted into the seventeenth and eighteenth centuries.

The second moment of major tension occurred in the nineteenth century when large swathes of the Muslim world fell under direct or indirect European hegemony. This political and military hegemony was accompanied by a sustained assault on Islam and Muhammad by what one might call the "Missionary-Orientalist" complex. As European orientalists of the nineteenth century acquired an unprecedented knowledge of early Islamic historical texts, it was not a difficult matter for them to cherry pick among these sources in order to construct a series of images of Muhammad and his religion depicting them as essentially violent and inimical to civilization, images that continue to thrive today among certain Evangelical circles in the Western world. A single quote from this literature will have to suffice, though this comes from a very influential work, Sir William Muir's *Life of Muhammad*, which first appeared in 1861: 'The sword of Muhammad and the Qur'an are the most stubborn enemies of Civilization, Liberty and Truth which the world has yet known.' Though such charges were familiar from premodern polemics, these charges by Muir were embedded in a carefully constructed historical narrative and would reignite an old and smouldering fire. The Muslim response was not slow to materialize and included Muslim writers and poets from India to Egypt. Several biographies of Muhammad, many of them equally polemical, now appeared and strove to rebut the charges of violence and barbarism, and scores of present day Muslim biographies of the Prophet are still haunted by this polemic.

What of Jesus in this encounter? In 1910, perhaps the most famous poet of his times, the Egyptian Ahmad Shawqi (1868-1932), upon whom the title "Prince of Poets" was bestowed during a pan-Arab cultural festival in 1927, wrote a poem called *In the Footsteps of the Prophet's Mantle*. This was a poem, some one hundred and ninety lines long, of praise of the Prophet modelled after an earlier pre-modern poem called *The Prophet's Mantle* by al-Busiri, an Egyptian Sufi who died in 1296. Both the original poem and Shawqi's echo of it became intertwined, each adding to the other's renown and popularity. Both poems belong to a genre of poetry in praise of Muhammad, and the later poem follows the earlier in structure, meter, rhyme and mood. However, about halfway through, Shawqi's poem of some 190 lines begins to allude to the political scene of its own days and finally faces contemporary western Christian attacks on the Prophet and answers them directly. Having first contrasted the raising of one dead man by 'your brother Jesus' with raising multitudes of the 'dead' in spirit by Muhammad, Shawqi proceeds to address a common charge against Islam:

> *They say: 'You conquered, but the Messengers of God*
> *   were not sent*
> *To kill souls nor were they sent to shed blood.'*
> *This is ignorance, misrepresentation, sophistry!*
> *You (Muhammad) conquered with the sword after you*
> *   had conquered with the pen. . .*
> *Evil, confronted with good, renders one incapable of*
> *   checking it,*
> *But, confronted with evil, it recedes. . .*
> *Had Christianity not had its protectors, brandishing*
> *   swords,*
> *It would not have benefited from its clemency and*
> *   mercy. . .*
> *It is the followers of Jesus who have now readied all*
> *   instruments of war,*
> *And we have readied nothing but weakness.*

This poem may serve as a convenient summation of the third period, described above as 'Jesus between east and west.' Polemic is by its nature reiterative, and Shawqi's poem recapitulates several polemical arguments of the pre-modern era. What is novel about it is the confession of Islam's weakness when faced with the 'followers of Jesus' who are now exposed as the true war mongers and hypocrites who preach mercy and practice violence.

If we accept the view advanced by Jaroslav Pelikan in his influential *Jesus Through the Centuries* that it was only in the nineteenth and twentieth centuries that Jesus became a liberator in western literature, this new image of Jesus was first clearly seen in the Arabic world in the mid-twentieth century.

Within one year of each other, two books that dealt with Jesus Christ written by two Egyptian Muslims appeared in Egypt and were widely acclaimed throughout the Arabic speaking world. These books introduced a "modernist" image of Jesus, which prepared the way for a revolutionary Jesus, a Jesus who was a hero of the spirit, a liberator of the wretched of the earth. The first book, published in 1953, was called *The Genius of Christ* whose author, 'Abbas Mahmud al-'Aqqad (1889-1964), had already established a towering reputation as a liberal journalist and prolific author on a wide variety of subjects both eastern and western. The second, published in 1954, was a novel called *An Unjust City* (entitled *City of Wrong* in its English translation) whose author, Muhammad Kamil Husain (1901-1977), was a renowned surgeon with deep interests in literature.

Al-'Aqqad, largely eschewing polemic and effectively ignoring the vast Islamic literature on Jesus, inducts Jesus into a series of biographies of "geniuses" that includes the Prophet Muhammad and his major companions. It is densely based on his reading of the Old and New Testaments and of some modern, mainly English, histories of the ancient world. 'Aqqad intends to summarize the significance of Jesus for 'Aqqad's own age, and *The Genius of Christ* is cast in the form of a quasi-academic account that inevitably, or at least naturally, leads to Jesus. The inspiration comes from Carlyle's *Heroes* on the one hand and from an older Islamic view that prophets appear when most needed by their times. 'Aqqad thus depicts the ancient world as one which was expecting a saviour and where petrified religions and materialistic and deeply divided societies were yearning for true faith, peace and harmony. In the introduction to the pre-Christian eras of history, which takes up almost half the work, generalizations are everywhere and allow 'Aqqad to exhibit to the full his rhetorical armoury, his neo-classical Arabic style and his own scholarly credentials.

About half way through, we finally come to the life and teachings of Jesus, which 'Aqqad describe as puzzling, amazingly novel and totally in contradiction to their surroundings. Like any genuinely new idea or calling, the teachings of Jesus impose an extraordinary burden on the believers, among which is the early call to his disciples to abandon all family ties. This, says 'Aqqad, is essential for any movement that seeks radically to oppose social, religious and political tyranny. The world of Jesus is a world of 'appearance without substance', of 'luxury and superficial belief' but without 'inward conscience'; it was a 'petrified' world where relations between races and sects were at their worst. A total revolution was thus required, and Jesus undermined the 'law of appearances' and introduced the 'law of love and conscience.' Jesus, says 'Aqqad, had taken a decision from the early days of his ministry not to draw near to power, yet a clash between them was unavoidable given that his worst sin in the eyes of authority was advocating forgiveness of sins and repentance – and these were the prerogatives of the powers that be. Jesus extended his most tender acts of mercy to women, the most unjustly treated of all classes, and consorted with the wretched of the earth.

Here then is a figure who radically overturns one law, that of hollow social forms and shells, and replaces it with the law of love, mercy and individual conscience. Though he promised his readers to make his account relevant to his day and age, 'Aqqad does not deliver on that promise. In only two instances does he turn his face to his immediate environment. In the first, he affirms that if Jesus were to return to earth, he would have much to do to reform his followers, many of whom have become like the Pharisees of old. In the second, he claims that the Egyptian bureaucracy of his days boast of their knowledge of the law but misuse this knowledge to manipulate or stupefy the ignorant, acting, once again, like the Pharisees.

The second work, *An Unjust City*, was equally celebrated in its day and age. It describes itself as a novel that takes place on Good Friday in Jerusalem, but might better be described as a combination of *roman à clef* and *pièce de theatre*. The cast of characters is fairly large, a mixture of New Testament and fictional figures, all of whom reflect from various standpoints on the meaning of that momentous day but without an appearance by Jesus himself. Each character is assigned a chapter where he or she, in conversation with others, expresses a range of ideas and emotions centring on the imminent crucifixion. We first meet a young Jewish prosecutor who objects to Jesus for treating all men as equal while his wife defends Jesus. Other pretexts for the crucifixion are offered such as the danger that Jesus represents to the Jews in confusing their received ideas, the social instability that his teachings foment and the heretical nature of his views. Next comes Caiaphas, the high priest, who is full of confusion and moral doubts regarding Jesus, and while he regards his existence as a danger, he nevertheless acknowledges his innocence. Then there is a debate in the Sanhedrin, where arguments flow back and forth; eventually it is decided that the teachings of Jesus are too sublime for ordinary people to understand and, thus, are subversive.

The scene shifts to the Christian community where a meeting of the Apostles discusses whether to save Jesus by force, setting up a pretext for the discussion of violence vs. non-violence, means and ends, truth vs. power, the goodness of God vs. the world's evil and individual vs. communal ethics. Finally, we hear from the Romans, who represent the primacy of the *imperium*, of discipline and order, and voices are heard arguing for and against just war and the true meaning of courage.

The *roman à clef* had been popular in Arabic literature particularly since the work of Taha Husain entitled *'Ala Hamish al-Sira* ('On the Margins of the Prophet's Biography'), which first appeared in 1933, a semi-fictional reconstruction of Muhammad's life. To borrow the technique of the novel in order to deliver a political and ethical message was one way to circumvent the Muslim and Christian religious establishments in Egypt, perennially powerful and easily excitable, particularly when the subject of the "novel" was a sacred figure. The fact that the author of *An Unjust City* was a liberal-minded Muslim added to its originality as a Muslim reflection on the meaning of the crucifixion, an event otherwise denied in the Qur'an.

Though very different in genre, both 'Aqqad's *Genius of Christ* and Kamil Husain's *An Unjust City* appeared at a moment in Egypt's history when, under British hegemony, Muslim-Christian unity was a central pillar of the nationalist platform. Both works revive a long tradition of Muslim reverence and love for Jesus, and reinforce it by making him speak for a wide range of political, theological and ethical issues. In 'Aqqad, the message is straightforward: we need to recapture the spirit of the law and to renew the struggle against the despotism of thought and political life. In *An Unjust City*, to kill Jesus is to kill conscience, the greatest of human catastrophes – and one that happens every day. A community has no conscience, hence will frequently be drawn to evil. Only the individual has a conscience, and the message of Jesus concerns the moral rebirth of the individual and the infinite mercy of God. 'Aqqad's Jesus is overtly political, Kamil Husain's more obviously ethical, but both see in Jesus a towering spiritual figure whose life and death carried many vital messages of rejuvenation for their own age.

4. Jesus the revolutionary

The last period in our survey is ushered in by the advent of modernist poetry. Round about the mid-twentieth century, the free verse movement swept over Arabic poetry, rejecting its meters and end-rhymes, and argued vigorously for a verse that drew inspiration from its own imaginative realm, unencumbered by rules of prosody. The movement's sources of inspiration cannot be dealt with here, but one constant and powerful source was myth. Why myth? The astonishing series of archaeological discoveries in countries like Egypt, Iraq, Syria and Palestine brought the ancient past and its myths into the immediate orbit of the poetic imagination. The rediscovery of the countryside and the rural origins of several of these poets, where very ancient customs still persisted despite centuries of Islamic or Christian rule, further advanced myth as an essential part of the human experience. Muslim poets in particular, in searching their own sacred revelation for mythical materials and in comparing myths, turn to Jesus as a figure more in tune with nature and the seasons than the explicitly and sternly anti-mythical figure of Muhammad. In exploring the world of myth, these Modernist Muslim poets saw Jesus, more than any other prophet, as an essential cusp in the mythical chain, a living figure through whom one must pass in order to recapture the conceptual and linguistic possibilities of myth. When evoking images of Jesus, these poets were not constrained by normal Muslim dogmas regarding his life, most notably the explicit Qur'anic denial of his divinity and his crucifixion. Instead, they felt free to introduce the crucified Christ into the fabric of their verse, almost provocatively, as if to insist that the images of his divinity and crucifixion are too precious to poetry to be abandoned for the sake of religious dogma. Putting it another way, one might say that, whereas the Qur'an and other sacred writings tilted backwards to the miraculous origins of Jesus rather than forwards to his Passion, the Passion of Jesus was essential to modern regenerative poets who wished to breathe new life into both language and society; poets, if you like, of resurrection.

For obvious reasons, Palestinian poets in particular found in Jesus a figure most befitting to express the tragedy of their loss and the hope for a rebirth of their homeland. The pathos, to begin with, is captured in a poem entitled 'To Christ the Lord on his birthday' by the poetess Fadwa Tuqan (1917-2003), excerpted here:

O Lord, glory of all creation,
On your birthday, this year,
Jerusalem and its joys are crucified.
On your birthday, all bells have fallen silent,
Bells that for two thousand years never ceased to ring
Except on your birthday, this year. . .
O Lord, glory of Jerusalem,
From the well of sorrow, from the pit, from the depth of night,
From the midst of woe,
Rises to you the wailing of Jerusalem.
Mercy, O Lord!
Let this cup pass from her lips.

Jerusalem's Passion terminates in the agony in the Garden, an agony to which the rest of the world is deaf. Other Palestinian poets, however, hear very different bells as in the two poems 'Bells of Christmas, 1971' and 'Bells of Christmas, 1974' by Ahmad Dahbur (1946-). In the first poem Dahbur evokes Christ as a Palestinian freedom fighter:

This night the bells tell me
Of a fighter whom children know,
In his hands are two nails,
Around him the fields grow large.
His face a beacon:
At one time shining, at another says 'No'.
When a helpless person among us pleads, he scolds him,
He orders him to rise, till even the lame shall run. . .
The bells will then tell me
That my hour has come,
That a Lord has descended from the cross,
His resurrection a joy to men and to the path,
And a city shall cry for joy.
The bells tell me that my grieving sister
Shall shed her mourning clothes
To follow him who walked on water,
And the dams shall open their floodgates to her,
And life will commence anew.

The second poem, a poetic evocation of the ministry of Jesus, ends as follows:

I heard the cock crow three times,
My memory is of cold and darkness,
My memory is of tin roofs and tents.
In truth I say to you: paths obscure shall confuse me,

143

And a difficult age shall challenge me. . .
The bitter cup shall not pass from me.
I will be doubted, my blood will be shed,
But I am the worshipper of revolution,
I cannot go back on eyes that spotted my dream,
I cannot go back on my poor.

Here the identification of the life of Christ with the Palestinian struggle and exile is explicit and complete, a sort of destiny.

The third Palestinian poet, Mahmud Darwish (1941-2008), enjoys a bigger reputation than either Tuqan or Dahbur. His poetry, at least his later poetry, is highly complex in its imagery and in its interweaving of symbols, almost irritating in their intricacy. In his poem called 'Leaving the Shores of the Mediterranean,' Darwish speaks of a Christ endlessly bleeding, endlessly struggling against the law of might, hosting in his cosmic body a never-ending stream of martyrs, a world-weary Christ. This is not so much Christ as patron of mercy or champion of revolution but rather Christ as a perpetual exile, bleeding so that others may live but alternately coming near and going far: a legend, indeed a language, that defies understanding:

Elegies are tired of victims,
And victims have frozen their sorrows.
Alas! Who will elegize elegies?
Poets, do not multiply!
My wounds are not a journal.
Leaders, do not multiply!
My bones are not a pulpit. . .
Sleepers of the Cave, come forth
And crucify me yet again.
Try to shed your names and you will find my hand,

Try to shed your clothes and you will find my blood. . .
Come gather around a legend:
Short of a miracle, you will not understand me,
For your languages are clear
And clarity is a crime. . .
Do not stop me from bleeding.
The moment of birth haunts me from all eternity;
Come find rest in my wounds.
Here's a homeland about to be renewed,
Here's a homeland about to be glorified.

This is the Christ of the eternal return: forever crucified, forever renewed, forever beyond understanding. Eventually, the theme of exile wraps up this strange and complex poem.

In Gaza, time clashed with space.
Its fishermen wasted their last chance to wash my feet.
Where is Mary Magdalen?
Her fingers dissolved with the soap,
And flowed out in writings, writings,
While soldiers were conquering, conquering.
They searched fingernails and toenails for a
*   guerrilla's joy,*
And coupled Magdalen's life
With the tears of Hagar. The desert was perched on
*   my skin.*
The first tear on earth was an Arab tear.
Do you remember Hagar's tears—the first woman to cry
*   in a never ending exile?*
O Hagar, celebrate my new exile, from the ribs of
*   the tomb*
Up to the universe where I rise.
Martyrs dwell in my unconfined ribs.

Then I lay bare the graves and Mediterranean shores.
Come celebrate my new exile!

The fourth poet in this survey is the Sudanese Muhammad al-Fayturi (1936-2015) whose poem 'Resurrection' (*Al-Qiyama*) might be described as a hymn or else a song of yearning for the second coming of Christ. Fayturi first addresses Christ as follows:

O human, god, prophet ! From us come offerings and
     yearning,
From you grace and glad tidings.
A desert of bronze we are were it not for you,
Eras made of stone.
From the hell of ritual, from the tracery of words,
From the cyclical seasons,
The roofs of our temples and the food of our tables,
We bow in never ending prayer, on pools of blood,
That spread over our arms and our silken pillows.
Defeats penetrate us, running away from the eyes
Of him who shall come,
While we cover up our sins which the eyes of mothers
     reveal.
Blessed be your steps,
You who shall come to this earth, piercing the mountain
     of secrets,
Your sacred halo surrounds you,
The glory of the heavens enfold you.
You come as you did before
To wash away our crimes and our sterility.
Here you are, solicitous for your dead,
Shaking from their bodies the dust of years,
Blessing their days as you turn towards us,

August in your sorrow.
Your heart breeds no resentment,
Your glory inherits no death,
Your face wears no arrogance.

The poem then goes on to say that Christ cannot be confined to myth or art or some image in scripture but exists in all creation, like a universal soul, and ends with a prayer:

O divine human!
You who conquered hatred, death and pride,
Smile upon those who ended in you
And those who began in you.
Say your word, be a hope to them,
Answer those who ask you,
You who offered your blood as a gift,
A wine, a salvation to their souls,
And wept over those who killed you!

To my mind, however, it is the Iraqi Badr Shakir al-Sayyab's (1926-1964) poem 'Christ After the Crucifixion' which captures most memorably the fascination of modernist Muslim poetry with the images of Christ. This is a poem that has received considerable critical attention and has obviously entered the canon, but for that very reason it can always bear more readings. With apologies to those who know it well, and apologies also to the Muse of Translation, I turn to examine it in some detail.

The poem is a monologue and Christ is the speaker throughout. It is divided into eight stanzas of unequal length, eight consecutive visions. It has a spectacular, apocalyptic opening:

After they brought me down, I heard the winds
In a lengthy wail, rustling the palm trees,

And steps fading away. So then, my wounds
And the Cross upon which they nailed me all afternoon
    and evening
Did not kill me. I listened. The wail
Was crossing the plain between me and the city
Like a rope pulling at a ship
As it sinks to the sea-bed. The dirge
Was like a thread of light between dawn and
    midnight,
Upon a grieving winter sky.
And the city, nursing its feelings, fell asleep.

The second stanza evokes Jaykur, the poet's home village, but expanded 'to the furthest reaches of fancy', and ready to receive the reviving sun, water and earth that constitute the body of Christ, which becomes the loaf of bread endlessly baked in the fire to give life, and the blood flowing in the veins of its earth. It ends as follows:

I was in the beginning, and in the beginning was
    Poverty.
{kuntu bad'an, wa fi'l bad'i kana al-faqir}
I died that bread may be eaten in my name; that they
    plant me in season.
How many lives will I live! For in every furrow of earth
I have become a future, I have become a seed.
I have become a race of men, in every human heart
A drop of my blood, or a little drop.

The poem now suddenly changes register, and redemption turns into nightmare. There is first an abrupt, hallucinatory, encounter between Christ and Judas Iscariot, with something of the atmosphere of Christ and the Grand Inquisitor in Dostoevsky's

The Brothers Karamazov. In the name of tradition, Judas rejects the risen Christ and says to him:

> *Is it you? Or is that my shadow grown white and scat-*
>   *tering light?*
> *Do you come back from the world of death? But death*
>   *comes once.*
> *This is what our fathers say, thus they taught us. Was it*
>   *a lie?*
> (Fa hal kana zura: a phrase with a gloriously Qur'anic
>   ring)

The nightmare intensifies. Christ entombed is now invaded by marching feet, by soldiers breaking in on him:

> *They took me by surprise*
> *As a palm tree in fruit*
> *Is surprised by a hungry flock of birds*
> *In some abandoned village.*

A cosmic battle ensues between fire and iron on the one side and the light shining in the eyes of 'my people', made up of memories and love, which carry 'my burden so that my cross becomes moist'. The stanza ends with a paradox:

> *How small was that death, my death, and how vast!*

The very last stanza recapitulates the first:

> *After they nailed me and I cast my eyes towards the city*
> *I hardly recognized the plain, the wall, the cemetery:*
> *As far as the eye could see, it was something*
> *Like a forest in bloom.*

Wherever the eye could reach, <u>there</u> was a cross, a
  grieving mother.
The Lord be sanctified!
This is the city about to give birth.

There is much to be said about this poem, like all poetry which is perpetually seductive. In brief, what we have here, first of all, is a poem of exceptional purity of syntax and diction, a poem whose diction and internal rhyme scheme is as strict as any diction or rhyme in a classical Arabic *qasida,* or ode. It is a poem of salvation, political and theological, a poem that interweaves, in an apocalyptic voice, both the crucified Jesus of the Gospels and the risen Christ triumphant, a Jesus who is Lord of the wretched of the earth and a Christ who is Lord and healer of nature. It makes a distinct theological and political statement about Christ to which one suspects many Christians would assent. It is a passion in miniature or even an apocalypse of the sort one might find in some apocryphal gospels.

What we have here in this long tradition is something approximating what might be called a love affair between Islam and Jesus. It is an instance, certainly unusual in the history of comparative religion, whereby one religion reaches out to adopt the spiritual founder of another religion in order to expand and reinforce its own piety. This record has something to teach us about how religious cultures in general did, or perhaps even ought to, interact, enrich themselves and learn to coexist, to become complementary.

When we contemplate the contemporary tension between Christians and Muslims, it is salutary to remind ourselves of another age and another narrative when Christianity and Islam were more open to each other, more aware and reliant on each other's witness – indeed, still are, when we see many of the most celebrated Arab Muslim poets of our day continue to turn to

Jesus for their imagery and their inspiration. And by way of contrast, when we examine the arguments put forward by proponents of the "Clash of Civilizations" theory, we might point to the danger inherent in this terrible misuse of metaphor. Armies clash, nations clash, peoples clash, interests clash. But do civilizations clash? Given this long record, it may be more appropriate to speak of the "Dance of Civilizations", "The Waltz of Civilizations", even of their "embrace", as has been attempted in this essay.

The genius of ambiguity

JULIAN BAGGINI

No one really knows who Jesus was, what he said and did, or even whether he really existed. Countless scholars have attempted to prove otherwise, but none has come close to a widely accepted reconstruction. Faith may be enough to fill the gaps in this knowledge for many Christians but for the rest of us, the historical Jesus remains an enigma. And yet this same Jesus is worshipped as the founder of a religious movement that by some margin has more followers than any other on earth.

This is no paradox. My contention is that it is precisely because the historical Jesus is so opaque that the religion that bears his name has been so adaptive to survival and growth. Whether Jesus was an actual, single person or not, what he represented was both powerful and malleable enough to sustain two millennia of interpretation and evolution.

Many assume that Jesus must have been a real historical figure, even if many of the tales told about him later in the Gospels have been fabricated. It is odd that so many non-Christians believe this given that they (and a great number of Christians for that matter) believe the Gospels are full of fictions. The healings, miracles and eventual rising from the dead are not little dramatic flourishes scattered around to spice up the texts. They are core parts of the narrative. Why should we assume that such a concocted tale has a real historical figure as its central character?

There is in fact surprisingly little evidence for his actual existence – less surprising once you consider how scanty contemporaneous records of anyone other than the great and the good around that time are. He is mentioned in the Jewish historian Josephus's *Antiquities of the Jews* (c. 93–94 CE) and the Roman historian Tacitus's *Annals* (c. 109 CE), and even these were written half a century after his supposed death.

Some naively believe that Jesus' life and teachings were so singular that they could not have been stitched together from fragments of other philosophies, theologies and biographies. History suggests otherwise. As Runar M. Thorsteinsson's eye opening *Jesus as Philosopher* persuasively argues, there is hardly a single teaching found in the Gospels which is not at least very similar to others in wide circulation in the Graeco-Roman world of the time.[1] Nor was the age short of people believed to be the messiah, or of Jewish leaders crucified by the Romans for allegedly stirring insurrection.

So the most likely answer to the question of who Jesus was is that he is a hybrid character forged from a variety of lives and teachings. At some point, a nascent religious movement curated these diverse elements to create their version of Jesus.

If this is right, then the origins of the Jesus we know prefigured the uses that would be made of him in the future. Jesus has always been a figure open to interpretation, almost infinitely malleable, becoming whatever versions of the Messiah are needed in different times and places, even closely contiguous ones. The wealth-endowing Jesus of the prosperity gospel dwells across the road from the humble ascetic Jesus of the Quakers. The gay-hating evangelical Jesus is worshipped next door to the Episcopal Jesus who doesn't care what your sexuality is. As Albert Schweitzer wrote, 'each successive epoch of theology found its own thoughts in Jesus; that was, indeed, the only way in which it could make Him live. But it was not only each epoch that found its reflection in Jesus; each individual created Him in accordance with his own character.'[2] Although all thinkers and religious leaders have had their teachings interpreted in diverse ways, the Jesus of the Gospels is surely the most fertile source.

It is tempting to see the interpretative fecundity as a product of Jesus' paradoxical nature – at once fully human and fully divine. From this other seeming paradoxes follow: powerless and all-powerful, a leader and a servant, mortal and immortal. Jesus is often both/and, rarely either/or, which opens up myriad interpretative possibilities. However, we should always be wary of neat dichotomies. The genius of the character of Jesus is not that he occupies pairs of opposite positions, but that he can be placed in any number of positions along the whole spectrum between two extremes.

Take his divinity and humanity first. Over millennia, Christians have traditionally seen him as having both properties. But that is where the consensus ends. Some see his divinity as foremost, others his humanity. More recently, some have gone so far as to see his divinity in purely metaphorical terms. Nor is it even necessary to settle on one view. The same church, the same believer, can choose to see him as more human in some cases and more divine in others, depending on what is most useful in the context.

I'm not suggesting that this interpretative flexibility is cynical or even deliberate. It is rather that the contradictory nature of Jesus more than makes it possible; it actively invites it. As Kierkegaard so beautifully explained, from a logical point of view, no one can be both fully human and fully divine. 'That God has existed in human form, has been born, grown up, and so forth, is surely the paradox *sensu strictissimo*, the absolute paradox.'[3] So to accept that Jesus was just this requires a leap of faith beyond rationality. Once this leap has been taken, the demand for logical consistency is left behind. Anyone who has taken it can move from human-Jesus to divine-Jesus in a heartbeat.

This makes Jesus particularly attractive as an object of veneration. On the one hand, his humanity invites the possibility of a personal relationship. This is arguably one of the great innovations of Christianity. Previously, your relationship to God was entirely vertical and mediated through the tribe or group, via a priesthood. Christianity introduced the possibility that anyone could come to God through Jesus, not just Jews but Romans, Samaritans or any other kind of Gentile. And because Jesus was a man, the relationship could be on a more human level.

On the other hand, as God, Jesus can also inspire awe and reverence. He can strike fear into you, act as the omnipresent policeman and judge. Yes, he was a man, but not a man like any other.

You can see this interplay between Jesus-as-fellow-human and Jesus-as-divine-other in forms of worship. In many more evangelical services, preachers talk to Jesus as though he were another person in the room. At the same time, their words and demeanour make it clear that he is not *just* another person in the room. Still, it is telling that in such denominations the divine trinity is frequently addressed as Jesus rather than as God. In more conservative, hierarchical denominations, Jesus is addressed more formally and less frequently, since the God part of the trinity is emphasized more.

The god/man nature of Jesus allowed diversity in branches of Christianity and heterogeneity within them. Christians could take a pick-and-mix approach, opting for awesome divinity or approachable humanity as it suited. No other religion has such a flexible figurehead. Islam has an entirely human prophet and a somewhat remote and fearsome God, who demands submission as an object of worship. Buddhism contains both naturalistic and supernatural strands, but the Buddha himself is an exceptional human being, no more.

The multiplicity of Gods and the abstract, divine Brahman in Hinduism allows some ambiguity, but nowhere near as much as Jesus.

The all-things-to-all-believers nature of the god/man Jesus opens up other spectra of interpretation. For instance, he is sometimes a leader, sometimes a servant, sometimes both. This ambiguity reaches its zenith in the Gospel of John, where Jesus puts himself squarely in the role of leader: 'You are my friends if you do what I command you.' (John 15.14) Yet in John 13 Jesus takes on the role of servant, washing his disciples' feet. But as he explains to them the meaning of what he has done, he makes it clear that he is still superior to them. 'You call me Teacher and Lord— and you are right, for that is what I am.' (John 13.13) His point is that even a master and lord must serve. This does not mean that no master is greater than his servant, but only the asymmetric claim that, 'servants are not greater than their master'. (John 13.16) If the master can be so humble as to wash another's feet, a servant certainly should be too.

Jesus radically revises the master-servant relationship without abolishing it. In doing so, he makes the roles of leader and servant ambiguous. This is something he repeatedly does. In John 15 he tells his disciples, 'I do not call you servants any longer, because the servant does not know what the master is doing; but I have called you friends, because I have made known to you everything that I have heard from my Father.' (John 15.15) Superficially, this looks like he has made them his equals, but given what he has already said, that is impossible. He remains first among equals, a friend, but also the leader of his friends.

The ambiguity of Jesus also plays out along a spectrum of helplessness/omnipotence, suffering/curing. The symbol of Christianity came to be the cross, a constant reminder of Jesus' human suffering. There is no other major religion that has as its central motif the weakness and pain of its central figure. Yet, of course, on the third day he rose again. The suffering on the cross is not erased, but it is more than balanced out. Nor was there any doubt Jesus had powers if he chose to use them. He is reported to have performed many miracles, walked on water and even raised Lazarus.

These passages show how Jesus can be seen both as the master and servant, lord and friend, mighty and humble, vulnerable and omnipotent. Again, this is very helpful to his reception in future generations. He can appeal both to those who like to look up to an awe-inspiring sovereign and to those who prefer a more humble, egalitarian form of leadership. So, for instance, Christianity could thrive both in its nascent days when it faced persecution from the Roman authorities and when it became the official state religion of the former oppressor. Today, Christianity survives as the major religion in many countries where the faithful can see their dominance as fulfilment of Jesus' prophesy to Peter that 'on this rock I will build my church, and the gates of Hades will not prevail against it.' (Matthew 16.18) In other parts of the world, believers face discrimination and even persecution, taking comfort in the fact that 'Blessed are you when people hate you, and when they exclude you, revile you, and defame you on account of the Son of Man. Rejoice in that day and leap for joy, for surely your reward is great heaven.' (Luke 6.22-23)

The duality of suffering and healing has played out over the years most obviously in the literal sense of physical health. Christians have tended to believe in the power of miraculous healing. Around six million pilgrims visit Lourdes every year, and prayers for healing are a part of almost all church services. Yet if people do not get better, they do not blame God for they know also that those who weep and mourn are blessed, and their reward will come.

Many of the diverse interpretations of Jesus' teachings and example are understandable, even inevitable, given their ambiguity. But others exploit this ambiguity to go beyond what any reasonable interpretation allows. The duality of power and powerlessness in particular has enabled Christianity to thrive in the ways that reflect most badly on it. For all the ambiguity of his teaching, there is little to no doubt that the Gospel preached a gentle asceticism at the very least, certainly no more than material modesty. Jesus was also anti-clerical. He told his followers, 'you are not to be called rabbi . . . and you are all students. Nor are you to be called instructors . . .' (Matthew 23.8; 10) It's also as clear as can be that Jesus preached non-violence, perhaps to the point of complete pacifism. 'for all who take the sword will perish by the sword.' (Matthew 26.52)

The power Jesus had was not the kind of power we associate with secular kings, barons and billionaires. 'the Kingdom of God is among you.' (Luke 17.21) It is not any kind of worldly empire. Jesus showed no interest at all in political power, refusing to lead an insurrection. He called his followers away from such concerns to something both higher and inner. 'Then give to the emperor the things that are the emperor's and to God the things that are God's'. (Luke 20.25)

Yet the church that was founded in his name has frequently held and used political power, and amassed tremendous wealth. It has supported wars, often of conquest, and even practised torture and execution. Parish priests have preached the Gospel of the poor to the poor while popes and bishops have passed their days in opulent palaces. Grand cathedrals to the glory of God have been built by the poor with the benefaction of the rich while the poor were left to live in penury. Ways of parting the faithful from their money have always been found, with pilgrims providing easy pickings. Lourdes, which has the second largest number of hotels in France after Paris, remains a shabby example of this, with its tacky souvenirs such as a "Miraculous Handbag Mirror" and an "illuminate Musical Angel Snow Globe".

Such exploitations of ambiguity, far beyond what reasonable interpretation allows, can happen for two reasons. First of all, the appeal of a religion depends more on the big picture than any fine details. In broad brush terms, there is almighty power to behold in the Jesus story. He came, after all, as a king and died hailed a king. Why shouldn't his church be mighty?

The second factor is that there are just enough of Jesus' phrases that can be appealed to in order to support many distortions of his overall message. The pacific Jesus can be ignored in favour of the one who said, 'I have not come to bring peace, but a sword.' (Matthew 10.34), never mind that in context this is clearly metaphorical. The Jesus who abhorred riches can be turned into the founder of the prosperity gospel, promising that 'For to those who have, more will be given, and they will have an abundance.' (Matthew 13.12) Selective distortion of quotations of sacred texts is not a vice restricted to Christianity. What makes the twisting of Jesus' purported words especially powerful is that it takes place against a background of radical ambiguity in the teachings themselves, thus making diverse interpretations of what would otherwise be plain misrepresentations more plausible.

At different moments of history, different elements of Jesus' ambiguity become more salient. In recent decades, his stance on sex and marriage has been centre stage. It has been the battleground on which many intra-denominational feuds have been fought between conservatives and reformers. If Jesus had any clear teachings on this subject, the debates would not have even been possible. But as with so much,

Jesus is enigmatic, ambivalent to the point of seeming to be contradictory.

Conservatives are able to point to some proclamations which support what they see as traditional family values, but which are actually much more historically contingent social and moral norms. His teaching on divorce was stricter than that of his time: 'Anyone who divorces his wife, and marries another commits adultery, and whoever marries a woman divorced from her husband commits adultery.' (Luke 16.18) What's more, you didn't even have to do anything to be guilty of the sin. Having the wrong desire is sin enough: 'everyone who looks at a woman with lust has already committed adultery with her in his heart.' (Matthew 5.28)

There is also grist for the mill of those who insist that Jesus made no room for anything other than heterosexual unions. In Matthew (19.4-6) he says, 'Have you not read that the one who made them at the beginning "made them male and female," . . . "For this reason a man shall leave his father and mother and be joined to his wife, and the two shall become one flesh"? So they are no longer two, but one flesh. Therefore, what God has joined together, let no one separate.'

However, liberals can point to the fact that he said very little about sex and marriage. True, he was clear about divorce, but as to what the unmarried can get up to, he was silent. By his behaviour, it was clear that he took a relaxed attitude to perceived sexual immorality. He saves an adulterous woman from stoning by asking her accusers if they were without sin. This seems to treat her own transgression as no more or less serious than any other. He also consorted with prostitutes.

Liberals are also helped by one of Jesus' most useful invitations to interpretative freedom. More than once he claims both to be upholding the old law while clearly changing it. He is able to do this by appealing to the spirit rather than the letter of the law. 'The sabbath was made for humankind, and not humankind for the sabbath.' (Mark 2.27) He says this in defence of his disciples threshing corn in their hands to eat, seemingly breaking the rule not to work on the Sabbath. As part of their defence, Jesus gives the example of David 'when he and his companions were hungry and in need of food . . . He entered the house of God, when Abiathar was high priest, and ate the bread of the Presence, which it is not lawful for any but the priests to eat, and he gave some to his companions.' (Mark 2.25–26)

In this and many other places, Jesus suggests that how we apply the law varies according to circumstances. What matters most is being true to its intention, which is to serve our best interests. If we accept this, it is not so difficult to see how sexual morality can also evolve. In a poor community where sex tends to result in pregnancy, there is no abortion, and children are needed to look after their parents, it is natural that sex is restricted to marriage and homosexuality is seen as a kind of indulgence. In an over-populated world with plentiful contraception, these considerations don't apply.

Of course, Jesus said nothing about this. But it is precisely because he said so little and invites interpretation that we can now offer this and many other interpretations, safe in the knowledge that nothing can be said decisively against us. As with other aspects of his teachings, it is not a crude matter of Jesus being capable of being used to support liberals or conservatives. Any shade of interpretation in between is also possible.

Perhaps Jesus' most potent ambiguity concerns how open or closed his Gospel is. Religions tend to thrive by creating a division between in- and out-groups. Believers are inside, part of a close community, pitted against unbelieving, sometimes hostile, outsiders. At its best, this dynamic creates community and solidarity; at worst it creates hatred for others and a simplistic division of the world into the righteous and wicked, the saved and the damned.

This closed aspect of religious sects, however, can act as an obstacle to growth. It is difficult to stay welcoming and open when you are teaching division and opposition to those outside the group. So there is a tension between remaining open and therefore able to grow and remaining closed enough to give the movement identity and cohesion.

The major religions of the world have confronted this problem differently. Islam grew initially by conquest: outsiders were forced to become insiders. Conversion played a role in later years, but the greatest expansions have been top-down. In Indonesia, for example, Islam was established for many years as a minority religion by Arabic traders, but it was the expansion of Islamic Sultanates in the fifteenth century that consolidated its grip. It is striking that Islam has not managed to grow significantly by any means other than Muslim rules expanding their dominion. The world's Muslim population has increased in recent decades without such expansion, but only because of the relative youth and high fertility rates of Muslims. According to a report by Pew Research, religious conversion is not a factor since 'the number of people becoming Muslim is roughly offset by the number of people leaving Islam'.[4]

The major religions of India offer two contrasting models for survival. Once it was established in the Indian subcontinent and some parts of southeast Asia, what we now call Hinduism settled for consolidation. It has never been a proselytizing religion but endured because it had a large community of believers. Buddhism, the relatively new upstart religion, was not able to challenge Hindu dominance on the subcontinent, but it managed to grow by exporting itself. Like Christianity, its success in doing so was in part down to it being adaptable. The versions of the religion in different parts of Asia are all different, absorbing and transforming preexisting belief systems to fit in.

Of course, Christianity's growth has not a little to do with conquest and colonialism. But I would suggest one factor in its success is its ability to play both the open and closed cards, sometimes at the same time.

This dual nature is evident in the teachings of Jesus. On the one hand, his is a gospel open to everyone. 'Come to me, all you that are weary and are carrying heavy burdens, and I will give you rest,' he says, adding, 'For my yoke is easy, and my burden is light.' (Matthew 11.28; 30) The rhetoric of openness is also found in sayings such as 'In my Father's house there are many dwelling places'. (John 14.2) No one is excluded from salvation: Gentiles, Romans, tax-collectors, prostitutes – all are welcome.

And yet it is not difficult to find plenty of other passages that suggest following Jesus means joining a tight in-group, in conflict with the hostile world. The nearest expression of this is when he says, 'If the world hate you, be aware that it hated me before it hated you. If you belonged to the world, the world would love you as its own. Because you do belong to the world, but I have chosen you out of the world—therefore the world hates you.' (John 15.18-19) There are many teachings, which say clearly that most people will not follow the true path to salvation, such as 'For the gate is narrow and the way is hard, that leads to life, and those who find it are few.' (Matthew 7.14) And, of course, there is the exclusivist verse beloved of evangelical posters, 'I am the way, and the truth, and the life. No one comes to the Father except through me.' (John 14.6)

Different denominations can play these open and closed cards in their own way. Jehovah's Witnesses are very skilled at playing both. On the one hand, it is a very tight-knit community, which demands service and obedience to strict teachings. On the other, everyone is sent out to evangelize, opening the door for others to enter in. This is simply the most vivid example of a duality common to many Christian denominations. Inside, there is a strong sense of being an in-group, but not only is the door open, people are actively encouraged to enter.

There is another, related spectrum that has become particularly useful in the modern age. Christianity emphasizes the community of believers, but it also stresses the individual's relationship to God. Christian life is communal, but salvation is personal. This gives it the capacity to appeal both to our desire for belonging and for autonomy and individuality. In the modern, developed word this is very important. Personal choice is highly prized, but people have not lost the need for connection. Christianity can give you both, and again, the wide choice of congregations means that each can find something close to the balance of collective and individual that suits them.

I say 'congregations' rather than denominations because the diversity within denominations is sometimes overlooked. When I grew up, as a Roman Catholic, we had two churches we could go to in our town. One was sober and austere; the other was best known for its bar where the priests would happily share a dram with their flock. Again, this shows Christianity's genius for diversity, made possible by the fundamental ambiguity of Jesus.

Beliefs have been compared to genes, each having a different survival value based on its capacity to reproduce fitness to survive, and to viruses, which need to "infect" their carriers, who then pass them on. Both these metaphors are flawed because genes and viruses mutate only slowly and have a singular form at any one time. The metaphor that best explains Christianity's ability to spread and survive is the one of supply and demand in the economic market. The demand for religion comes from many sources: desire for belonging, identity, reassurance, life-guidance, ritual. Successful suppliers meet these needs. Sometimes, these suppliers enjoy local monopolies by crowding out competitors and being strong enough to see off upstarts, most of which are simply not as attractive. Sometimes a monopoly is enforced by the state, just as Soviet regimes offer their populations just one brand of soap powder. In a free market, competition intensifies. But markets do not usually fragment as much as might be expected. Rather, the big brands get better at market segmentation, offering different varieties of pasta sauce.

From the outset, Christianity was more adept than any other religion at making sure its product line appealed to a wider set of spiritual seekers than any competitor. It could do this because the heart of its brand was a mythical figure who could be placed at either end of various spectra of religious belief and practice, and at any point in between. This allowed the message of Jesus not only to appear in different forms at the same time, but also to evolve over time, adapting to changing social and economic conditions. At the moment, for example, we're seeing teachings on gender equality and sexuality change more in decades than they had over centuries. That would simply not be possible if Jesus had left us with a clear set of teachings.

The market metaphor should not be taken too literally. It is simply a vivid way to make clear how Jesus' enduring power derives from his capacity to be whatever a leader, community or individual needs him to be. The ultimate genius of this is that when you know which Jesus is yours, he doesn't seem a particularly enigmatic or ambiguous figure to you at all.

Each hears him speak clearly, but each hears him speak differently. It's a difficult trick political parties have been trying to pull off for decades. That Jesus does it so well is little short of miraculous.

Notes

The genius of ambiguity

1 Runar M. Thorsteinsson, *Jesus as Philosopher: The Moral Sage in the Synoptic Gospels* (Oxford University Press, 2018).
2 Albert Schweitzer, The Quest of the Historical Jesus (A. and C. Black, 1911), p. 4.
3 Søren Kierkegaard, Concluding Unscientific Postscript, trans. David F. Swendon and Walter Lowrie (Princeton University Press, 1968) p.194
4 The Future of the Global Muslim Population. <https://www.pewforum.org/2011/01/27/the-future-of-the-global-muslim-population/>

Jesus and the beginnings of Christian theology

ROWAN WILLIAMS

Once upon a time, theologians spent a lot of time and energy on the question of the relation between "the Jesus of history" and "the Christ of faith". What was the link between the life of a first-century Jewish artisan and the conviction of biblical writers like Paul and John that Jesus was the embodiment of a divine Wisdom in which the universe finds its coherence? Perhaps if we could excavate enough material about the Jewish artisan we could in some way assess the credibility of the claims around the figure of incarnate Wisdom; we could assess whether the historical facts could in any way "justify" such an ambitious metaphysical conclusion. And if it proved impossible – or if it were in principle impossible – to recover such historical material, then surely the most we could say was that some inaccessible set of events somehow prompted the appearance of a new religious movement. That movement might or might not attract our allegiance, but such allegiance could not be anchored to any claims about its actual origins; any doctrinal affirmations about the figure at its centre could only be – at best – imaginative projections.

If the landscape of theology now looks rather different, that is not because we have managed to access a lot of clearer evidence about the Jewish artisan or even about his first followers; it is more to do with the recognition that the polarization we started with takes for granted a view of history that is very hard to defend – an assumption that there is somewhere a record of the past from nobody's point of view – and a view of metaphysical/ mythical discourse as some sort of explanatory thesis. But the problem is not that the history of Jesus is difficult to access, overlaid as it is by the literary and theological reception of his story; in one important sense every historical figure is a literary figure, encountered through the medium of how others made sense of them. And if we begin where we have to begin, from the earliest written testimony to the life of Jesus, what is striking about the record and recollection of him is that these narratives and allusions, from just a couple of decades after his crucifixion, are already freely using the language of the embodiment of divine Wisdom (as, for example, in the opening chapters of Paul's first letter to Corinth). It is not as though we could reconstruct a steady accrual of theological elaboration around a simple story, or a series of puzzling historical data in search of an explanation. The "sense" that was being made of the memory of Jesus by his followers was, from very early on, bound up with the picture of Jesus as enacting and transmitting the activity of the creator; and it was thus bound up with the conviction that Jesus' own activity had not ceased with death (as expressed in the ensemble of not always clear and consistent stories in the Gospels about his resurrection). It was not a gradual extension of metaphysical explanations or clarifications.

This is not meant to be some sort of shortcut, claiming that we have only to take on trust this developed "making-sense" and ask no questions about the specifics of the world in which Jesus of Nazareth lived and died. It is simply to note that Jesus first appears as this kind of "literary" figure – not as a martyr or prophet in conventional guise, but as someone whose agency is inseparable from that which actively holds the universe in being. If we want to interrogate what lies beyond this (startling) representation, the answer is not to be found in the search for some uncommitted and uncompromised evidence, but in attending to the way in which early Christian language about Jesus foregrounds certain themes in the story: how it continues to carry the marks of stresses and discontinuities; how its own persistent untidiness works to convey the nature of the question that Jesus' life and death was experienced as posing.

If that sounds a bit too much influenced by fashionable theories of interpretation, perhaps the simplest way of putting it is to remember that there are four Gospels: for some reason, the telling of Jesus' story never settled down in one authoritative version. Each apparently coherent and theologically shaped version of the story was read and transmitted – again from very early on – in conscious dialogue with others, as if no one account of the story would suffice. The slight but significant shifts of focus between the versions become part of the "canonical" deposit: this is a narrative which is hard to finish either telling or hearing, as the conclusion of John's Gospel suggests. 'Jesus did many other things as well', says the evangelist, and if all were recorded, 'the whole world would not have room for the books that would be written.' (John 21.25) It is as if the acts of Jesus would necessarily exceed the limits of the world; as if any telling of this life short of this would be inadequate. The Gospel text itself does its work by insisting that it is incomplete.

A story of fulfilment and disruption

One thing we might say about this historical figure whom we cannot clearly see is that, for whatever reason, he generated for those around him a particularly acute problem about how he should be spoken of, because the response to his acts and words unsettled some important conventions of speaking or narrating. The New Testament writers view the story of Jesus as one of fulfilment: this is where a long history comes to its proper conclusion, both interpreting and being interpreted by its narrative background. But they also see it as a story of disruption: this is a shattering and remoulding of the background. In terms of the narratives of the Gospels, we see how the events of Jesus' life and death are described as "fulfilling" narrative foretypes in Jewish scripture or fleshing out prophetic metaphors. Jesus is presented in ways that echo the stories of Moses or David or Elijah or Jonah, and he is explicitly claimed to be the actual historical correlate of the prophecies of a victorious liberator. At the same time, one of the prophetic foretypes regularly invoked is that of a divine word or invitation that is ignored, misunderstood or rejected; those who have the language and "mythical" repertoire to make sense of his life do not respond, or they respond with hostility (John 1.10–11). The focal tension is expressed in Paul's letter to the Christians of Galatia, when he boldly addresses the most traumatic moment of disruption, the execution of Jesus: this too is a "fulfilment", but of the most bizarre and contradictory kind. In Jewish scripture, the enemies of God's people are to have their bodies publicly exposed and hanged on a tree – and the one who is supposed to embody God's unchanging and transforming friendship towards this people suffers precisely this punishment. He dies under a curse (Galatians 3.13).

From the very beginning this tension transformed itself into a story not only of disruption but of negation: Jesus is rejected by God's people, who are in turn rejected by God in favour of those who *do* respond in trust to Jesus. Christian scripture itself is marked by this seductive simplification, and the burgeoning ferocity of Christian anti-Semitism over the centuries is a hideous reminder of where such simplifications lead. Yet the central gospel narrative itself and much of the earliest reflection do not make any such move. It seems that one thing we have to conclude about the figure "beyond the narrative" is that he did indeed (like many earlier Jewish prophetic critics and renewal movements) provoke debate about the calling and integrity of God's people in his context; but it was the history and vocation of this people that conditioned his own teaching and activity. We know from many other contemporary sources that this was a time in which several attempts were made to rally the Jewish people in some kind of newly united identity against their own corrupt elites or against the Roman occupying armies, or both. Jesus dies by the means of execution normally allotted to rebels, indicating that the Roman administration saw his actions as another effort at such a "rallying" of Israel. Yet there is very little indeed to suggest that he engaged in the large-scale, direct and sometimes threatening protests that some others orchestrated.

One clue to untangling this can be found in the persistent tradition in the narratives that Jesus deliberately associated with disreputable, marginalized and non-observant individuals (mostly Jews but occasionally Samaritans or Gentiles); that he resisted the rigorous application of purity regulations; and that his "rallying point" was simply an appeal to trust his announcing of God's amnesty and welcome. It sounds as though Jesus was in effect saying to his Jewish contemporaries: *A life-and-death upheaval is drawing close, and there is an opportunity for the people of God to come together afresh and rediscover their true identity – an identity that is completely dependent on the free forgiveness and hospitality of God.* It is not a matter of ethnic solidarity alone, nor is it something earned and maintained by legal scrupulosity alone; it is not an identity secured by a political concordat with an oppressive imperial power. In other words, it is exactly what the Torah says it is: the assembly of those who respond to the free determination of God to call human beings into a relationship in which God commits to mercy and renewal – a "covenant" relationship, created by God alone. This is the heart of the story of Abraham and Moses; what Jesus challenges is not the calling of Israel but the reduction of Israel's identity either to just another political phenomenon or to a community of those who believe they are somehow uniquely qualified to receive God's grace.

Jesus is reported as saying that he has no intention of minimizing or overthrowing the tradition; rather, he is saying two interconnected things. First, the identity of God's people is that of a community whose integrity and rationale lie simply in the act and summons of a merciful God. This is the "kingdom of God", which Jesus proclaims as on the point of appearing in its fullness – the space in the human world and human history where God's sovereign will is manifestly the determining reality. It is the vision set out eloquently in the book of Deuteronomy: 'Has any God ever tried to take for himself one nation?' (Deut.4.34). This is an identity bestowed, not acquired. For the community to live by this conviction is for it to show the world the nature of the God it speaks of: the God who is not to be deflected from the divine purpose by human failure and who is completely unconstrained in realizing that purpose by any kind of finite limitation.

Second, Jesus is saying that in a time of impending crisis for God's people, it is essential to bring this sense of divinely bestowed identity back into the centre of Jewish self-understanding; and this is both symbolized and effected by Jesus through his dramatic reaching-out to and standing alongside those who know they cannot acquire what is needed to belong fully to the people. The tension between Jesus' insistence on fidelity to the Law and his risky involvement with those widely seen as "lawless" is something in the Gospel narratives which cannot be avoided, and certainly cannot be properly rendered as a programme of replacing Jewish identity with something alien.

We cannot be certain whether Jesus had any consistent attitude or programme in respect to non-Jews, though there are reports of his individual interactions with a good many of them, suggesting that he did not regard them as, by any means, outside the scope of divine mercy. It was left to the first generations of his followers to take the difficult and problematic step of concluding that the definitions of God's people might now extend to non-Jews. The New Testament writings again bear the marks of a complex and sometimes bitter set of arguments about what this might mean and what it might practically entail. Christian scripture thus tells us obliquely, by recording the kind of arguments that took place in the early Christian communities, what the issues were that were generated by Jesus' actions and sayings.

So the perspective that comes into view in the early days of Christian language and practice is that of a community that is an intensified and unboundaried version of Jewish identity – that is, a community wholly depending on divine calling. It is no accident that the term the first Christian communities used for themselves was the Greek word conventionally used to designate the assembly or convocation of all Israel, the assembly of those "summoned" or "called": *ekklesia* – a word which also designated the citizens' assembly of a Greek city. In other words, Jesus' dramatic acting-out of a kind of redrawing of the frontiers of God's people had within a couple of decades produced a community that was deeply puzzling to the authorities of the Roman world – a sort of "city", a sort of "people", yet without the expected external markers of identity: not claiming to replace or rival existing political realities, yet relativizing them by affirming a quite different level of loyalty and solidarity within a community presenting itself as a renewed humanity.

No ordinary death

As well as this complex balance between disruption and fulfilment, there is a further and immensely important theme in the Gospel narratives: Jesus remains active in the world; he is not dead. And he acts not only to bring his followers into a new relation with one another in the renewed community we have been thinking about, but he also acts so as to bring them into an identity with himself, in the sense that his followers are enabled to address God as he did and to act on his behalf in the world.

And so another tension is set up. If Jesus' ministry centred upon the claim to embody the divine calling to become God's people, the conviction that his execution did not end this embodiment gave to the figure of Jesus an authority that was of a different order to that of any human teacher. We are on the way to the characterization of Jesus as the embodiment of divine Wisdom, the ordering and reconciling power by which the universe coheres, the continuing presence of God's free act in the form of a human agent.

At the same time, the followers of Jesus are invited to share the unconditional dependence of Jesus on the God he addresses as 'Father'. The survival in the early Greek literature of the Aramaic word *Abba* as Jesus' form of address to God suggests a strong traditional recollection of Jesus' own usage. His liberty to speak on behalf of the divine creative liberty is balanced by a form of prayer that underlines the absolute derivation of this liberty from its divine source. Jesus does not claim an unusual degree of human spiritual power or supernatural skill but a direct continuity with the activity of God, which is realized only in a relation of loving and attentive dependence on God. Gift and response meet in Jesus; and as the history of Christian reflection unfolds, this meeting produces the elaborate and strained formulations that attempt to set out what it means to identify Jesus as equally "human" and "divine", and to speak of God as intrinsically and eternally constituted by relationality.

So if we want to look beyond the "literary" figure, it seems we are bound to posit a complicated relation with Jewish identity, and in particular a distinctive style and vocabulary of prayer, along with a structured and complex story about Jesus' death and what followed. This is not to seek some kind of objective grounding in historical fact for the faith expressed in the scriptural writings, only to try and imagine what made possible the kind of language we find in those writings. At the heart of it all is the fundamental Jewish idea of a community that finds its unity only in dependence on the commitment of God; a community therefore that challenges any version of "optimal" human identity and solidarity dependent on achievement, social homogeneity or systems of human political control. This 'kingdom of God' is not to be realized by human effort or human success: it becomes manifest in certain kinds of human life in common – hence the "'beatitudes'" in the Gospels of Matthew and Luke, declaring that those who live in single-minded devotion to God's justice, to peacemaking and humility, those who make themselves vulnerable for the sake of peace and forgiveness, are 'blessed', in harmony with God's purpose, and so are a place where the kingdom becomes visible (Matthew 5.1–11).

This opens up the quite involved cluster of ideas and images that gather around the story of Jesus' execution. Again we have to recognize that within fewer than twenty years of the event, Jesus' crucifixion had come to be routinely interpreted as something imbued with transformative significance, opening up a new way of speaking to and about God and of connecting with one another as human beings. It was – at the most obvious level – seen as fleshing out the disjunction between God's action and human power or success: in a world like this, a life lived in radical dependence on God is a life stripped of ordinary and prudent forms of human protection. The sheer difference of the kingdom of God is dramatically expressed in Jesus' apparent defeat, humiliation and killing. In John's gospel, this is articulated clearly by Jesus himself in the dialogue with his Roman judge, Pontius Pilate: 'My kingdom is not of this world. If it were, my servants would fight to prevent my arrest by the Jewish leaders' (John 18.3). But this is not all. We have already seen that Paul picks up the provocative idea that Jesus takes on the identity of an accursed enemy of Israel through his crucifixion. His acceptance of his death – and death in this particular form – is understood as one aspect of his identification with and assumption of the guilt of the rebel against God, the one who fights against the covenant. He takes on the punishment and curse of those who refuse what God gives, thus releasing those who literally refuse God from the consequences of their guilt. This builds on the remembered saying of Jesus that he would give his life as a 'ransom' – that is, he would risk death as a way of liberating others.

Thus, the crucifixion becomes, not exactly the simple substitution of an innocent victim for a guilty one to satisfy an abstract justice (the popular version in some kinds of Christianity), but the "diversion" of a chain of consequence so as to rescue others at risk. Declaring the paradox that the person must be fully in tune with the loving purpose of God should be stigmatized as the archetypal enemy of that purpose is a way of dramatically focusing the "inversion of values" that the preaching of Jesus announces.

But there is still more: the creation of a community living by the covenant of God's promise is, in Hebrew scripture, sealed by the sacrifice of an animal – and is also, in the theology of Jewish liturgy, grounded in the readiness of Abraham to sacrifice his son Isaac, an event commemorated daily in the worship of the Jerusalem Temple. The death of Jesus – associated in Matthew's gospel with the tearing of the sanctuary veil in the Temple – comes to be linked with the idea of a "new covenant", a new and more radical affirmation of God's faithfulness and accessibility. The wording of the ritual of the Lord's Supper, the community meal of bread and wine established by Jesus on the night before he dies and described by Paul in his first letter to Corinth, refers explicitly to the idea of an outpouring of blood as in a sacrifice that seals and confirms the divine covenant. And one further elaboration, alluded to by Paul but central to the involved theological scheme argued in the anonymous letter to "Hebrews", is the linkage of Jesus' death with the ritual of the Day of Atonement in the Temple: the day when the High Priest goes behind the sanctuary veil to sprinkle the blood of sacrifice on the Ark of the Covenant, which is the throne of the invisible God. The writer to the Hebrews interprets this as the presenting to God of the fleshly life of Jesus, representing the whole of humanity, as an offering that renews and restores the "flow" of God's mercy towards humankind, a once and for all "covering over" of the guilt of human beings by means of the self-giving of Jesus.

We can see from this very brief overview how the execution of Jesus stimulated an extraordinary range of interpretative exploration – how early reflection on what the events of Jesus' life and death "made possible", resulted in a diversity of readings and understandings. This is hardly surprising: Jesus' death is not straightforwardly that of a "martyr", dying for the sake of an established traditional and collective identity, or dying for "liberty" in the face of an oppressive alien force. As far as we can disentangle the detail of the Gospels on this subject, he is condemned according to Roman law for some kind of sedition, with the connivance of an influential group from the Judaean political elite. But this means that Jesus is not a "prisoner of conscience"; he is not like the Maccabean martyrs of Jewish tradition who die for refusing to compromise with pagan pressure to betray their faith. He is the victim of a piece of hasty improvisation by vested interests and of the mixture of indifference and political cowardice displayed by Roman officialdom. Both Judaean and Roman elites appear in the story as obsessed with public order and the defence of their status; but this makes the death of Jesus at first sight little more than another example of the anonymous brutality of imperial rule. If it has a distinctive meaning, this has to be sought elsewhere, and the early Christian communities sought it in the rich texture of Jewish liturgy combined with the archetypal myth of the victim who offers their life for the community's survival.

We see, then, that the death of Jesus was understood as an intrinsic, even necessary, aspect of the way that divine agency is at work in the human story of Jesus so as to create the renewed community of God's people. The rather bewildering range of narrative and metaphor used to make sense of the crucifixion of Jesus reflects in a very acute form the point already noted about the way early Christian writers seem unable or unwilling to settle for one definitive version of the story of Jesus. If Jesus is what he is claimed to be, they imply, a single fixed perspective will not do justice to the reality.

Why does Jesus still matter?

In conclusion: how does all this illuminate the basic question of why Jesus "matters"? For Christian believers, locating themselves within the renewed community that depends completely on God's act and invitation, the answer is clear enough: this life and death and resurrection definitively break through all our self-created ventures in providing ourselves with an identity. It confers on us the gift of standing where Jesus stands before God the Father, sharing – so far as finite subjects can share – his intimacy with the source of all, and his authority to remake human society through healing and mercy. But tracing the contours of the earliest responses to Jesus may help simply to bring into focus what was distinctive in this moment in the story of how humans understand themselves and their shared life. Two themes emerge with some clarity. Both can be expressed as questions rather than "theses".

The first is the question posed initially by the overall Jewish narrative of which Jesus is a part: what does a human society look like when its identity and coherence are understood as simply given in a way that imposes no humanly devised entrance requirements, no record of ancestry or achievement and no imperative to compete successfully against rival communities? There is an invitation to imagine the connectedness of human beings as a kinship that relates us all equally to something beyond all human negotiations of power and interest; as a community where value does not depend on successful performance of any kind, and where every contingent boundary between human groups must be understood and evaluated in the light of this. However badly this has been realized historically by the Christian Church – and the record might charitably be described as uneven – the logic of the narrative continues to be set out in the story the Church tells in its Bible and its sacraments; and it is a logic that has over the centuries generated a remarkable degree of human consensus – such that questions about the status of children and women, the legitimacy of slavery and the obligation of rich to poor, simply could not be discussed today on the same basis they would be (and were) in a world where Jesus had not existed.

The second theme is represented by the question posed in the story of Jesus' death as mediated and explored in the literature written by his early followers. In the light of this story, we are not only invited to imagine a community that does not depend for its stability or security on human power; we are invited to step further, to imagine that those who have experienced loss, powerlessness and victimization are the proper focus and test for any scheme of human meaning. To put it more simply: there can be no viable philosophy of human society that regards humiliation and exclusion as ignorable or inevitable or justifiable. The "mythic" assertion, the claim of faith, is that God is to be found in complete solidarity with those who suffer. For the person who is unclear about God, it is still possible, in the light of the story of Jesus' execution, to see suffering as having an unqualified claim on our attention and response. We are answerable to and for any kind of outrage against the human. This is why it is important – odd as it may sound – that the story of Jesus' death is not an edifying tale of martyrdom; its central figure is not a hero of conscience, but first and foremost a victim of self-interested power (religious as well as political). To put it another way: you do not have to be a hero for your suffering to be morally significant, or for this suffering to claim attention and effective love.

For the Christian, these perspectives – and imperatives – are rooted in the belief that the identity of Jesus is the identity of God as active in our world; and in the practice of the Church's sacraments they continue to open themselves to the same radical and transforming agency that was at work in the days of Jesus' life, trusting that this life remains the vehicle of God's own act, now as then. Belief in the resurrection is not to be reduced to a belief that a strange event happened long ago; it is a belief that Jesus never ceases to be the conduit for God's invitation to belong with God's people. On this basis, Christians will – can we say this? they don't always – see their witness as part of God's building up of a human community without boundaries, where the dignity of every human subject is honoured. At the same time, Christians will – can we say this? – seek to intensify their awareness of the perspective of the powerless and forgotten. Realizing this calling is, as we have already noted, something that looks pretty patchy in the history of the believing community, but the miracle is that the memory and re-presenting of Jesus' story and identity is not silenced, inside or outside the Church.

We have been trying to see how Christian scripture tells the story of Jesus in a way that points us to the elusive events beyond it, not by a simple photographic representation of those events but by telling the story with certain tensions and silences and unresolved paradoxes still plainly visible. This we see in the diversity of the four primary narratives, the painful interweaving of continuity and conflict with the Jewish story; and we see it in the embarrassment of a death that will not fit any edifying pattern, yet lends itself to any number of theological resonances. Whether you believe this or not, the scale on which the person of Jesus disrupts our clichés and assumptions about ourselves and our shared human life is still something that is capable of provoking wonder and even radical change: the switch of mindset that Christian scripture calls *metanoia*, repentance.

Index

Index

Index

Index